Wade and Kayak Fishing On Galveston Bays and Sourrounding Areas, 3rd Ed.*

by Ray Crawford

*Formally: Honey Holes Of Galveston Bay

Texas Coastal Fishing Books
Friendswood, Texas

Fishing
on
Galveston Bays
and
Surrounding Areas, 3rd Ed.*

by Ray Crawford

*Formally Honey Holes of Galveston Bay

The author has extensively researched the information contained in this book and he has tried his best to insure that it is accurate and up to date at the time of printing. He assumes no responsibilities for changes in wading or kayaking areas due to weather, currents, or changes in local ordinances and laws, nor for omissions, errors, or inaccurate descriptions.

Cover illustration by Ray Crawford

Map Drawings by Ray Crawford

All location photos by Ray Crawford unless otherwise noted.

Helicopter photos by Curley Myers

Satelite photos furnished by:
    (1) Texas General Land Office
        (a) 2002, aerial infrared (IR) color digital images
        (b) 2002, black and white aerial photos
        (c) 1999, color aerial photo of the south jetty.
    (2) Texas National Resources Information System
        (a) 1996, 1 meter digital orthophotos

Published by Texas Coastal Fishing Books; Friendswood, Texas

Printed by Sheridan Books; Ann Arbor, Michigan

ISBN 0-9742253-0-4   19.45

Acknowledgements

I would like to think my good friend Curley Myer, AKA hook m up, on the CCCF internet site, for taking the helicopter aerial photos that appear in this book; I would not have been able to afford them otherwise. I would also like to thank the Texas General Land Office for supplying the (1) 2002, aerial infrared (IR) color digital images, (2) 2002, black and white aerial photos, and (3) 1999, color aerial photo of the south jetty. (http://www.glo.state.tx.us/coastal/photos/) In addition I would like to think the Texas National Resources Information System (http://www.tnris.org/website/Allsids/) for supplying the 1996, 1 meter digital orthophotos. This wouldn't be complete unless I thanked my wife for putting up with stacks of paper I generated in researching the book and for tolerating the countless hours I had to spend on the computer.

This book is dedicated to the memory of my
grandfather, John Wade Crawford,
who came to Houston in a covered wagon.
He never had a lot of money, however he
loved hunting and fishing. He always had
time to listen to my problems and
his advise was always sound.

Table of Contents

North (Upper) Galveston Bay

West Shoreline, Mid-Galveston Bay

Areas Around the Causeway (I-45)

Galveston Island

West Bay to Brazos River

Quintana Jetties & Brazos River Area

Introduction

The Author, Fly Fishing in Jones Lake.
Photo by Kyle Crawford.

Fishing Strategies

I do not claim to be an expert fisherman, however I usually catch my share of the fish. There are several things I try to do the day before I go fishing: (1) I check the internet for the weather, the current water conditions, and the saltwater fishing boards (check the appendix for the URL's of most of the local sites), (2) I look in the *Gulf Coast Fisherman Magazine* for the times of the greatest current flow, and (3) the evening before I go, I call several marinas, piers, and bait camps in the area I plan to fish. This information gives me a good idea of what to expect when I get there, and if the conditions at this particular location are not favorable for fishing, I can then make an intelligent secondary choice. When I was younger in the late 50's and 60's, I got turned off of saltwater fishing because there was not any reliable way to check on conditions. This resulted in my making many unproductive trips to the coast when conditions were less than optimal. With today's technology, there is not any excuse for letting this happen. Of course, there are still those times when I have to get out of the house and go fishing, no matter what the conditions, just to keep from going crazy.

The keys to successfully fishing any of the places mentioned in this book, are: 1) understanding the proper use and rigging of your fishing equipment in targeting specific fish, 2) tide movement and especially current flow, 3) bait movement, 4) wind direction and velocity, 5) finding structure, and 6) if you are using artificials, locating water that is relatively clear. I have listed these in what I consider the order of importance, and if you were to ask someone else, you would probably get a different order of priorities.

I will defer the subject of what equipment to use to another forum. There are many excellent books, magazines, and internet sites that can give all the advice you need to get started. The internet is an excellent source for this information; post a question on one of the fishing boards listed under "Checking for Current Conditions" in the Appendix. While many anglers will not divulge their honey holes, they will gladly give advise on what equipment to use.

In general, the stronger the current flow, the better the bite, and the best source I can find that gives a breakdown of time and location for strength of current is the *Gulf Coast Fisherman Magazine.* It has a complete three month forecast of both the tides and **detailed tables on when the greatest current flow occurs.** A strong tide movement is sometimes a determining factor on which day of the week I go fishing. You can catch fish at 12:00 noon in the summer if there is a strong enough current. Baitfish and shrimp are moved in and out of the estuaries at the will of this current and you will find that predators will have their greatest feeding activity during this period. An incoming tide will push bait onto the flats and back into coves, while an outgoing tide will pull bait off the flats and to the mouth of coves and creeks. Of course it is possible for the current to be too strong on that particular day for the location you have chosen to fish. Areas such as a pass or cut to the gulf can have extremely strong and fast currents, which not only makes them unproductive to fish but also dangerous to wade. In this case, you simply need to move further back into the bay system where the strength of the current will be diminished.

The presence of baitfish is important for any successful fishing trip. Look for "nervous" water: water that has a lot of dimples or very small wavelets that have a different pattern than that produced by the prevailing wind. Jumping mullet will sometimes signal a predator is near, especially if the jumps are erratic. In addition, look for small oil slicks, preferably about the size of a wash tub. Specs will regurgitate their food when they are in a feeding frenzy and this creates an oil slick with a smell that many people describe as being similar to watermelon. With time, the oil slick enlarges; it may start out as small as a washtub and end up as large as a swimming pool or house. Therefore, the smaller the slick the better, since this indicates that it was recently produced.

The intensity and the direction the wind is blowing is closely related to water clarity. Generally for the best conditions you want an east or southeast wind blowing no more than fifteen miles per hour. A wind from any other direction or with a greater force will tend to muddy the water. The surf usually muddies first, closely followed by the bay. However, even with adverse wind conditions a fisherperson can usually find fairly clear water. The immediate south shorelines of most of the bays will remain fairly clear even if the wind is blowing hard from the southeast. These areas will eventually get muddy if the wind blows long enough. At a time like this, you may want to look toward the east shorelines of Trinity Bay. A southwest or west wind will almost certainly muddy most of the bays, but you can still find clear water along the protected shorelines of Seabrook or along the North Jetties at Bolivar.

Another important consideration is the presence of structure in the bay or surf. Structure is anything that changes the bay bottom or the water column and allows the predator to hide or that gives the predator an advantage over their prey. Structure might be a rock, an

3

oyster reef, a pier piling or even an area where there is an interface between clear water and muddy water. Specs, reds, and flounder all like different kinds of structure. Flounder prefer to lie in ambush for bait fish so you are most likely to find them lying on the bottom at the mouth of many bayous, cuts and sloughs during an outgoing tide. Redfish will often prefer shallow water where they can root around for small crabs, shrimp, and worms. You will usually find specs away from the shoreline in the bay near deeper water where they will often orient themselves to channels (guts) that are perhaps only 8 to 14 inches deeper than the surrounding bottom. If there is sea grass growing on the bottom, look for clear spots about as big as a bathtub or smaller. Trout will wait in the surrounding grass for any prey that ventures into the clear area.

Coves offer some of the most diverse structure in the bay system. On an outgoing tide, I usually start at the back of the cove near the grass lines and work my way to the front of the cove. This is where a kayak is really handy, because at the back of the cove, the bottom is usually muddy and difficult to wade. As the tide rises, baitfish will seek shelter in the grass of the marsh shoreline. This area will usually be shallow, and will have numerous cuts and channels that funnels both water and marine organisms (baitfish, crabs, and shrimp) in and out with the tides. Redfish will often go up into the grassy area to feed as the incoming tide floods the shoreline. As the tide starts to fall, the reds and flounder will position themselves outside the cuts and channels so that they can intercept the baitfish and shrimp as they are pulled to deeper water. When I first arrive at an area I plan to fish, it often pays to sit quietly in my kayak to look for bait fish and to observe any patterns of activity. Many times I have noticed that flounder will feed when power boats use the canal leading out of **Lake Como**. It seems that their wake has the same effect as a fast moving tide, pushing bait fish toward shallow shorelines.

When the current increases on the outgoing tide and the water level starts to drop, you may want to move outside of the cove and fish any major cuts or guts that you can identify. Fish this area just as you did the sloughs in the back of the cove. There are additional structures to key on at the front of coves. One is the point of land that occurs at each end of the cove as it opens out into the bay; this area can be fished just like a point in a freshwater lake. Other structures that may be found near the front of a cove are small islands, sand bars or reefs that act as barriers and protect the cove. All of these areas can hold fish on an outgoing or incoming tide. The best advise is to find two or three areas that you like and learn them well; fish during different tides and in all weather conditions. Hard work and persistence will pay off on those days when other fishermen go back to the dock empty handed.

Pier and bridge pilings should not be ignored when fishing the shoreline because flounder, sheepshead, and drum can often be found feeding around them. Tidal currents will often wash out the sand/mud from around wood and concrete pilings, leaving areas where flounder can hide and ambush their prey. To fish these areas from a pier, lower your line straight down by the piling and drag or jump your bait or lure slowly around the perimeter of the piling. Start at the piling closest to shore and work your way down the pier, stopping at each piling. Lone pilings and private piers can be fished from a kayak or by wading, however please observe property rights and stay away from commercial fishing piers unless you have paid to go on the pier. One pier owner that I know of, turned the piers lights off when a wade fisherman was observed in the water taking advantage of the free light source.

The definition of clear water along the Texas coast is dependent upon where on the coast you fish. Along the upper coast, clear water may have one foot of visibility, while along the lower coast, this would be considered somewhat murky. Trout are known as sight feeders, so if a person is using artificials, the clearer the water the better. Redfish do not seem to mind muddy water since they spend most of their time rooting around the bottom like an armadillo or hog and in the process of their feeding, they create their own small area of low visibility. I have always felt that flounder were closer to trout in this respect, in that they are ambush feeders. A person using live bait does not have

5

to be as concerned about the water clarity because of the bait's natural scent. Look for water that has streaks of discoloration running through it and fish this interface between the muddy and clear water. This is excellent fishing "structure" for it gives the predator the concealment they need for ambushing prey.

Safety: Stingrays are a very big concern if you are wade fishing. I highly recommend some type of leg protection, however most waders opt to do the Texas two-step and shuffle their feet. Fishing from a kayak is another option, but if you ever get off the kayak, wade carefully. A person must get immediate medical attention after being struck by a ray. To lessen the pain, it has been recommended to immerse the area in hot water.

I believe that a personal flotation devise (PFD) should be worn at all times. Since I fish by myself a lot, I wear one every time I am on my kayak or out wading, and with the new suspender type of PFD's, I hardly know I have it on. Some places are more dangerous to wade than others, and San Luis Pass is one of these areas. Every year, two to four people lose their life while fishing/swimming around the bridge in San Luis Pass; the currents here can be treacherous. No one will take better care of your life than you; be careful and **wear the PFD.**

I want to make a few comments on the aerial photos and how to use them. **Figure 1 – page C1**, is a small section taken from the Christmas Bay, east end, IR photo, **page C22**. The photos originally were in an ECW format, averaging about eight hundred MB (0.8 GB), so it takes special software to view the images and also a fairly fast computer that can handle extremely large files. The images used in this book were converted to JPG and then digitally enhanced using Photoshop. For convenience, the exact same photo in grayscale is found on page 7.

Find Churchill Bayou and notice the extension of the bayou as a gut (**"A"** – the dark blue) into Christmas Bay. This area is deeper than the surrounding area and it acts as a thoroughfare for fish to use when entering and exiting the bay. It is a great area for locating flounder on an incoming tide. Another similar area is **"D"**, where a slough enters Churchill Bayou and an outgoing tide would concentrate flounder at the confluence of the slough and the bayou. You can also see the transition from shallow to deeper water, **"B"**, plus possible sand bars and/or reefs, **"C"**. The area below **"B"**, probably represents where the grass line stops. These details are found on most of the aerial photos and if studied carefully, a lot of useful information can be gained that would not be obvious to a fisherman/woman visiting the area for the first time.

One last comment: Due to the large number of fishing places mentioned in this book, some of them were not checked this year, but one or two years ago. This means that any strong current could have made new or deeper cuts in some areas and thus I am not aware of them. Therefore **always wade carefully until you learn the area (and wear your PFD).**

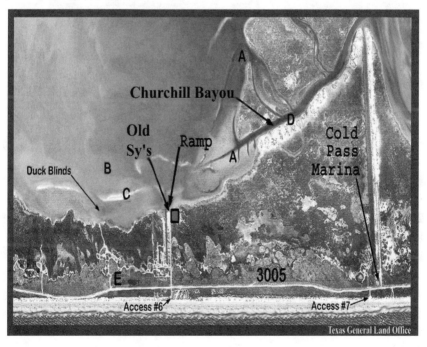

Places to Catch Baitfish in the Galveston Area

1. Cone Island Road is a great place to catch bait and also to fish for flounder/redfish. (See Figures 2 and 3) **Turn east onto Levee Road (Co. Rd. 690), and when it turns left, there will be a partially paved/gravel road on the right that will take you off the levee. This is Co. Rd. 891 or Cone Island Road.** Try any of the canals alongside or at the end of the road. If you launch your kayak here, be cautious of large boats or tugs because there is very little room for them to navigate.

Figure 2. Levee Rd. and Cone Island Rd, Surfside.
Photo by Curly Myers.

2. Many of the **estuaries** that are **parallel to the feeder or frontage road along I-45** driving into Galveston have a lot of baitfish. **There is a low bridge that goes over a small canal which passes under I-45 and then it flows out toward Jones Lake. Take Exit 6 from I-45 going south, or if you are on Hwy. 6, get on I-45 and then take Exit 6.** (See Figure 4)

Figure 3. Cone Island Rd, Surfside.
Photo by Curly Myers.

Figure 4. Canal at Exit 6.

3. There is an estuary on the north bound side of I-45, opposite the canal in #2, that at times holds a lot of baitfish (and also red fish and flounder). **Directions: going north bound on the Causeway, take the first exit on the mainland side of I-45.** (See Figure 5)

Figure 5. Estuary Opposite Canal in Figure 3.

4. One very popular site is the small bay at Exit 7 (Omega Bay) on the west side of I-45 (on the right if southbound).

5. Cold Pass, near the Bright Light Grocery store, at the end of the San Luis Pass Bridge.

6. At night, go to the bulkhead **inside the Brazoria County Park.** This is a very popular fishing place and if people are fishing, they probably do not want someone around throwing a cast net.

7. Under the SLP Bridge on the Follet Island side during an outgoing tide. The mullet will get into large pods and migrate out or, more likely, they are pulled out by a strong outgoing tide.

8. **At Surfside, before going over the tall bridge**, you will go over what looks like a levee with **a canal** that runs east and west (see #1). You can turn **right or left onto the levee road (Co. Rd 690) that runs parallel to the canal**. Often you will find a lot of baitfish in this canal. When I was a kid my parents would take me fishing here for reds and croaker. If the water is muddy everywhere else, it will be clear here.

9. There is a good chance of finding baitfish **in the sloughs along 332 in Surfside before you go over the tall bridge;** there are several of these on both sides of the road. I have caught bait **at the low bridge that is crossed just before reaching the tall bridge.**

10. **The Texas City Dike** can be an excellent place to catch mullet. Schools will often swim along the rocks about five feet out.

11. Try the **public boat ramp at Dickinson Bayou on Highway 146.**

12. **In the ditches at the very end of or along Sportsman Road.**

13. Try the **canal by the former site of the old abandoned condos on Christmas Bay.**

14. At the **mouth of the Brazos River,** there is a small cut or slough, upriver where live bait can be caught.

15. If you are fishing at **Fort Anahuac, look in the sloughs and canals close to the west side (right side facing the peninsula) boat launch.** Take the cast net and **go to the foot bridge and check here first. Another place to check is the shoreline on the right as you approach the boat launch.**

16. **On the east end of the Seawall Blvd., turn right onto Apffel Rd.** This is the road going to the condos near East Beach. After just a short distance, **you will cross a bridge separating two large lagoons or lakes** on both sides of the road.

17. Go east and at the end of the Seawall Blvd, turn right onto Boddeker Dr., which is the last road you can turn on before ending up in the ship channel. **On the left (east),** you will see a canal or lagoon that has a shoreline where it is easy to walk and use a cast net.

18. In Bolivar:

a. There is a small pond on the west side (left of the road if you are facing the small beach and bridge) of French Town Rd. This is the first road you can turn left onto, after you get off the ferry in Bolivar (for alternate directions, see **Bolivar and East Bay**). An alternate spot would be the body of water on the east side of French Town Rd. You can try the shoreline along this estuary or down at the bridge over the canal that drains this body of water. (See Figures 6 and 7)

b. After leaving the ferry, turn north on loop 108 at the blinking light. There is a bridge that allows drainage of the northern part of the estuary, about one half mile from the light. Try throwing your cast net here.

c. Across from the old lighthouse in Bolivar, there is a section of Hwy. 87 that passes right next to the gulf. The waves are never high because the area is protected from wind from all directions except due south. There is plenty of room to pull off the road and park. At times I have found pods of mullet along the shoreline or not far out.

Figure 6. Pond on French Town Rd.

DAILY BAG LIMITS[1]

Species	Daily Bag	Length in Inches (Min. - Max.)
Amberjack, greater	1	32 - No limit
Cobia	2	37 - No limit
Drum, black	**5**	**14 - 30**
Drum, red[2]	**3**	**20 - 28**
Flounder: all species,	**10**	**14 - No limit**
Mackerel, Spanish	**7**	**14 - No limit**
Seatrout, spotted	**10**	**15 - 25[3]**
Shark: all species	**1**	**24**
Sheepshead	**5**	**12 - No limit**
Snapper, lane	No limit	8 - No limit
Snapper, red	4	15 - No limit
Snapper, vermilion	No limit	10 - No limit
Snook	1	24 - 28

Bold Print = Species normally caught around Galveston Bay

1. Limits as of September 1, 2003.

2. One red drum over the stated maximum length limit may be retained when affixed with a properly executed Red Drum Tag and one red drum over the stated maximum length limit may be retained when affixed with a properly executed Bonus Red Drum Tag. Any fish retained under the authority of a Red Drum Tag or a Bonus Red Drum Tag shall be counted in addition to the daily bag and possession limit.

3. Only one trout over 25 inches can be retained.

14

BOLIVAR AND EAST BAY

1. Directions to the Ferry. (This is the long way, but the most direct and easiest to follow) Take **I-45 all the way through Galveston and turn left at Seawall Blvd. It is about 0.5 miles to hwy. 87 which is the turn off to the ferry. Turn left and get into the left lane to get on the ferry.** The shorter route would be to take **I-45 to Galveston and exit right at Harborside/Teichman. Go past the Strand and turn left onto Ferry Road.**

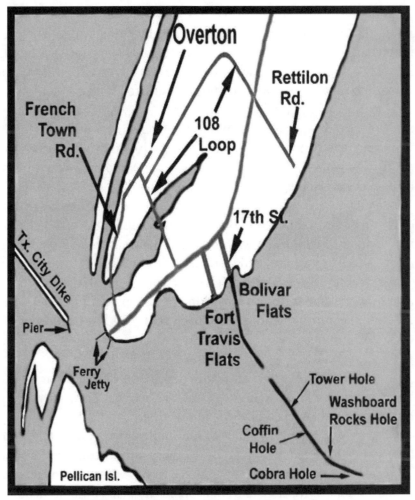

Figure 7. Bolivar. Not drawn to scale.

2. French's Rd./Cut. Directions: After you leave the ferry, turn left at the first road (0.2 miles). This is French Town Rd. If you can not make the first left due to traffic, go to the first blinking yellow light and turn left. This should be loop 108. It is 0.9 miles to Overton St. where you will turn left. This will take you to a small bridge with a beach which is excellent for wade fishing or launching a kayak. (See Figures 7, **8 – page C2**, and 21) A long, wide estuary, **Horseshoe Lake,** will be on the southeast side of the bridge.

The water can be swift as it passes under the bridge when the tide changes. This can make for some very good fishing on an outgoing tide on the bay side of the bridge. I have never fished here but Horseshoe Lake shows a lot of possibilities for someone willing to wade in mud; a kayak may be hard to use here except perhaps at high tide. French's Road is usually my back up that I use when I originally plan to fish the Bolivar Pocket and upon arriving, I find that it is too muddy. French's Road is protected from any wind that would make the pocket unfishable.

3. There are several options for fishing in the surf at Bolivar. Hwy. 87 parallels the beach all the way to where you must take a detour on hwy. 124. All of the sites below branch off of hwy. 87. I have included a large number of access points so that a surf or kayak fisher doesn't have to worry about driving down the beach and getting stuck. The further you get from the ferry and the closer to Gilcrist the deeper the water is close to shore.

a. The **Bolivar ferry jetties** can be outstanding during the flounder run in the fall. These are rock jetties that protect the ferry from waves and swells while it is in the process of docking and they are very close to the deep water of the ship channel. I am convinced these jetties have an advantage over other similar structures around Galveston, in that the prop wash from the ferries causes water currents similar to tidal movement and this sometimes will stimulate feeding activity. (See Figures **8 – page C2** and 9)

16

Figure 9. Bolivar Ferry Jetties.

b. There is a beach just to the right (south) after leaving the ferry. Go into the parking lot on the right, immediately after leaving the ferry, and walk back to the water just south of the ferry. On the south side of the rock groins that protect the ferry landing, there is a small beach that will allow you to access the water. Wade back to the south. This is an excellent place to catch flounder in the fall and winter. (See Figure **8 – page C2**)

c. Fort Travis Flats. The area to the west of the Fort, can be accessed shortly after getting off the ferry. The shore is lined with large rocks and there is good protection from west and southwest winds. I have seen people wading here, but I have never tried it myself. (See Figures **8 – page C2** and 10)

d. Ramp at North Jetty. 1.6 miles from the ferry, turn right on either 15th or 16th Street, and you will come to a small beach which is usually well maintained and it extends all the way to Fort Travis to the east, which is about 500-600 yards away. There is

17

excellent fishing in the area around the Fort, and the beach is perfect for launching a kayak if you do not want to use the ramp. (See Figures 11 and 12)

Figure 10. Beach West of Fort Travis.

e. North Jetty. A right on 17th St. will take you to the base of the North Jetty. (See Figures 13, **14 – page C1**, and **15 – page C3**) Both sides of the jetty can be waded, but expect to get into a lot of mud in many places on the left side. A kayak can be launched here but due to the cramped parking, I think the Erman Pilsner Ramp/ Beach is a better choice if you plan on fishing the **south side of the jetty**. The best place to launch a kayak or to wade and fish the **north side** is to continue to **Loop 108** and drive to the beach as described in **3.f.** below. The surface of the jetty is flat and it is fairly easy to pull a cart or cooler on it. The jetty is 5 miles long, however there is a boat cut 2 miles out from the base that keeps you from walking to the end.

If you are walking the rocks, it generally it is not worthwhile to fish the north side of the jetty until you get close to the boat cut. Most of this area is shallow and muddy, however the channels that the marsh in Figures **14 "A" – page C1** and **15 – page C3** should be a great place to look for flounder on a strong outgoing tide. Another area to try on the north side is about one hundred yards before you get to the boat cut where a deep hole has been gouged out by current that is funneled through the cut. This hole can be fished by kayak or by walking to the boat cut on the jetty. (See Figures **14 "C" – page C1** and **15 – page C3**). Do not overlook the many small guts that are formed along the shoreline, north of the boat cut. (See Figure **14 "B" – page C1**)

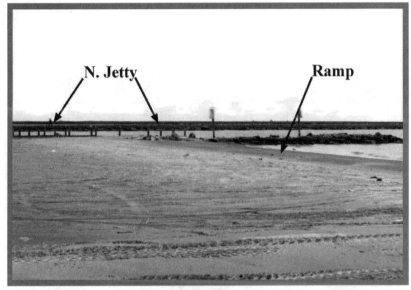

Figure 11. Ramp at N. Jetty.

f. 3.4 miles from the ferry, loop 108 crosses 87 and continues to the beach (Rettilon Rd.). Turn right at the beach and stop at the line of pilings ("rettilon" spelled backwards is "no litter"). This is where most people park to fish the **Bolivar Pocket** and this is a great place for launching a kayak or for wading. The waves are usually very small and the water is shallow for a long way out. Fishing can be outstanding whenever the wind is out of the west or southwest. There are usually a lot of small baby sharks ready to steal anything put onto a stringer, so I would recommend a long stringer or a floating basket. (See Figure **15 – page C3**)

Figure 12. Beach East of Fort Travis

Figure 13. North Jetties.

g. After you pass the brown water tank, there will be a large Bolivar Yacht Basin sign on the left. Turning right will take you to the beach.

h. 11.1 miles from the ferry, there is a sign on the right for Emerald Beach #2. The guts are deeper along this shoreline than most places in Galveston or Surfside. According to Joe Doggett, this is a site where old surf pluggers once fished, but today it has almost been forgotten.

i. Rollover Pass (See Figure 17 – page C4) **is 20 miles from the ferry** and it has excellent kayak launch sites from both sides of the Pass into **East Bay**. There are a lot of excellent flats to fish behind the Pass, however be careful of strong currents. When the current is moving, the water can be swift when it is funneled through the pass and there may be a few new holes that have been washed out. Another negative to wading the bay side is that the **Intercoastal Waterway (ICW)** runs down the length of the Bolivar peninsula, a short distance behind the pass, and this acts as a barrier to restrict waders to the south side of the ICW.

If you want to fish directly in the pass, just follow the example of most of the people who will have their car backed up to the barrier on both sides of the pass. Open up a lawn chair, pop the top of your favorite beverage and wait for fish to swim through. (See Figure 16)

When I fish **East Bay** behind the pass, I am usually in my kayak, and there are two places where I will launch depending upon the crowds. My first choice is directly behind the pass on the northwest corner. (See Figure 18) This allows me to fish the shallow flats and the pass channel that flows out to East Bay. If the pass area is too crowded, I will launch from a ramp into the ICW, a short distance west of the pass. (See Figure 17 – **page C4**)

j. Surf Side of Rollover Pass. While I love fishing the surf on Bolivar, I guess Rollover holds my interest more than any other place. The surf right at the pass can be dangerous, so I do not recommend wading anywhere in the vicinity of the mouth, however, several hundred yards in either direction of the pass, the beach has a hard sand bottom and it is great for wading. Almost any part of the beach can be used for launching a kayak. **Directions for getting on the beach: Turn toward the surf on either side of the pass and go past all of the parked cars, and there will be a sand ramp that will take you to the beach.** Keep in mind that this is a sand ramp and it is not always in the best shape and I have come close to getting stuck while trying to go up the ramp many times. (See Figures 19 and 20)

Figure 16. Rollover Pass, Southeast Corner.

Rollover is the main highway for fish traveling to or from the eastern part of **East Bay**. This fact can make fishing close to the mouth of the pass outstanding for specs, reds, and flounder. Fishing either from the beach or from a kayak, during an outgoing tide, resulted in some remarkable catches over the course of several years.

k. There are two last, good access points to the surf north of Rollover Pass. The first is 24.6 miles from the ferry and the

22

Figure 18. Rollover Pass, Flats Leading to East Bay.

second is 26.7 miles from the ferry. The state does not maintain highway 87 past the 124 cutoff, so if you go past this point, it is suggested that you have a four wheel drive vehicle. The **cow pens** that you may have heard of are several miles up the coast from this point.

4. Piers:

    a. Dirty Pelican Pier. 409-286-5854. Approximately 22 miles from the ferry. Live bait.

    b. Mecom's Pier. 409-286-5043. Approximately 25 miles from the ferry. Live bait.

Figure 19. Rollover Pass, SW Side.

Figure 20. Rollover Pass, West Beach.

5. Marinas and Bait Shops and boat ramps:

a. **Bolivar Bait Camp.** 409-684-4210. Boat ramp, live bait.

b. **Rollover Pass Bait and Tackle.** 409-286-5562. Live bait.

c. **Rock Bottom Bait & Tackle.** 409-684-7224. Boat ramp, live bait.

d. **Shirley's Bait Camp.** 409-684-8251. Boat ramp, live bait.

e. **Stingaree Marina.** 409-684-9530. Boat ramp, live bait.

f. **Tim's Bait & Tackle.** 409-286-5693. Boat ramp, live bait.

g. **Way Out Marina.** 409-684-3070. Boat ramp, live bait.

h. **Lauderdale Public Boat Ramp.** Public boat ramp just west of Rollover Pass on the ICW.

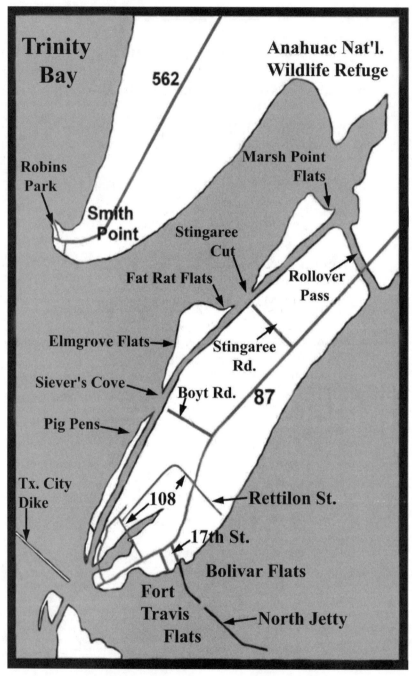

Figure 21. Bolivar. Not Drawn to Scale

East Galveston Bay

South Shoreline

1. Mouth of Saltwater Bayous. On an outgoing tide, fish the bayous and cuts that flow into East Galveston Bay on the south shoreline. Water flows out of the surrounding marsh and into the bayous, and baitfish are pulled out into the bay allowing trout and redfish wait to ambush them. Fish along the shorelines on both sides of the bayous.

2. "Hog Pens or Pig Pens". Launch your kayak at the Bolivar Bait Camp. **Turn left on Boyt Road from Hwy. 87. Sievers cut** goes through the ICW and takes you to East Bay. The **Pig Pens** are about ½ to 1 mile to the left. This area is really good on an incoming tide. Fish just east of the tall antenna tower; there are several guts that run along the shoreline as you wade further out from the bank. **Little Hanna's Reef** is about 1 mile to the right as you go through the cut. (See Figure 21)

3. Stingaree Cut. Look for Stingaree Road that is just past Crystal Beach. Go north through the cut and **Goat Island** will be on the right (east) side. You will see the ICW and the spoil islands to the right and left. Fish on both sides of the cut and around Goat Island and the ICW. Around to the left or west is **Fat Rat Pass** which is about a mile or so away. **Pepper Grove Reef**, **Middle Reef**, and **Deep Reef** are all easily accessible from the cut. These reefs are about .5 miles to the right from the cut. (See Figure 21)

4. Marsh Point Flats. This area can be reached by launching at Rollover Pass and going back to the left as you clear the ICW. Fish the spoil area immediately behind the Pass, especially the area by the ICW. (See Figures 21 and **22 – page C5**) The mouth of **Little Pasture Bayou** has yielded excellent catches of large specs during outgoing tides.

North Shoreline

1. Anahuac National Wildlife Refuge. (See Figures 23 and 28) **Directions: Take I-10 east to exit 810 (this is the Anahuac and Hwy 563 exit). Take a right on 563 and after 6 miles you will intersect hwy. 61 where you will turn left. Continue on 61 until you come to an intersection where 61 will turn left (north) back to I-10. Turn right to get on hwy 562 and continue on 562 for 8.5 miles. You will come to a fork and 562 will angle to the right to Smith Point. Instead of going right, take a left (east) at the fork and the road becomes 1985. About 4.2 miles from the fork there is an Anahuac Wildlife Refuge sign where you will turn right.** If you are coming from Bolivar, **take Hwy. 87 to High Island and turn north (left) at Hwy. 124. Turn left on 1985 and it is 10 miles to the refuge sign. The road into the Refuge is shell and it is 3 miles to the unmanned sign in station;** visitors must register as they enter.

Inside the refuge, go straight and the shell road will take you to East Bay. To fish Frozen Point, drive to the end of this road (about five miles), park at the locked gate, and it will be approximately another mile to the Point and three miles to Oyster Bayou. You can wade or launch a kayak anywhere along this shoreline, and expect to find excellent fishing with sand bottoms, grass flats, shell reefs and mud in a lot of places. As you get closer to Frozen Point, the mud gets deeper and I strongly recommend a kayak for this region. I have not fished the refuge in the winter, but I have been told by many that this is when the north shoreline comes into it's own since it is protected from a strong north and northeast wind.

The second road to the right will take you to a boat ramp that is one or two miles away from Robertson's Bayou which drains Robertson's Lake. There is plenty of room to park and the small launch ramp is on a short 30-40 foot cut or slough. All of the areas along this north shoreline can have excellent fishing for reds, flounder and specs. The bottom is mainly sand with some patches of mud and oyster reefs scattered throughout the area. If you catch your own bait, keep an eye on the many ditches that you pass along the shell road.

The north shoreline of **Trinity Bay** is a fantastic area to fish from a kayak because is not usually crowded and you don't have as many power boats, at least in comparison to West Bay. Plus the Frozen Point area is fairly muddy and a kayak is ideal in this type of situation. High tide at the eastern most part of East Bay is about 3 hours, 5 minutes later than the Galveston Channel tide.

One word of caution: This area is so isolated, that you need to be sure to let someone know where you are going and/or carry a cell phone, in case you have car trouble. It is a long walk out.

Smith Point

1. Smith Point, Robins Park. Directions: (See Figure 23) **Take I-10 east to exit 810 (Anahuac and Hwy. 563 exit). Take a right on 563 and after six miles you will intersect Hwy. 61 where you will turn left. Continue on 61 until you come to an intersection where 61 will turn left (north) back to I-10.** (An alternate route would be to stay on I-10 for another mile and take the very next exit; turn right on Hwy. 61.) **Turn right to get on Hwy. 562 and continue for 8.5 miles. You will come to a fork and 562 will angle to the right to Smith Point. To the left, the road becomes Hwy. 1985 and it will take you to the Anahuac Wildlife Refuge. Take 562 (to the right) and go to the town of Smith Point. Go through town and turn right at Hawkins Camp Rd. It is 15 miles from where 1985 branches off of 562 to Hawkins Camp Rd. Turn right and go 1.8 miles to Robins Park which will be at the very end of the road.** This road is mainly gravel, alternating with broken up blacktop.

When you get to Robins Park, all you will find is a restroom, an observation platform, and a very good boat launch. (See figure 24) The restroom is not in great shape at the present, and the

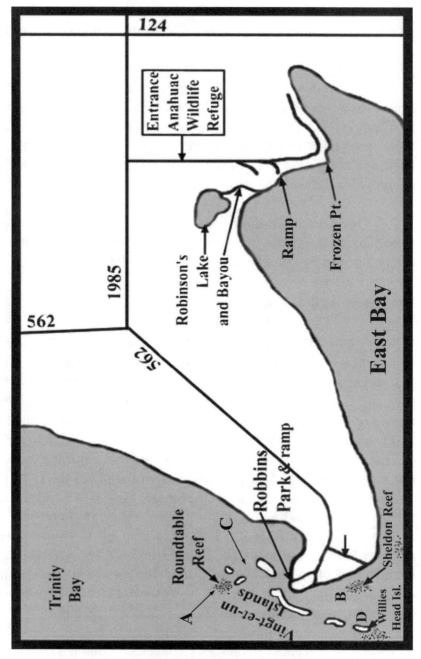

Figure 23. Smith Point and Anahuac National
Wildlife Refuge. (Not drawn to scale)

observation platform is missing the third story, however it is still functional. The second story of the platform allows you to get the lay of the land/water before heading out. If I have my kayak with me, I prefer launching from the shoreline, 20 yards to the right or left of the boat launch. Another option is to launch at the trailer park that you will pass just before entering Robins Park. I believe there is a small fee for using the ramp, but it has the added benefit is knowing that your car is probably safer.

Figure 24. Ramp at Robbins Park.

I get more excited about discussing Smith's Point than any other part of the Galveston Bay System. This area has more channels and bottom contour changes than almost any other place that I have investigated and they can all be located with a depth finder. Without a kayak, you can wade the Trinity Bay shoreline to the north or south, however be aware that there is a boat cut between the mainland and the islands.

There are several islands and channels to fish if you have a kayak. (See Figure 25) Look at the area labeled **"E"** in Figure **26 – page C6** and notice the small channel above the **"E"** that runs straight across from Robins Park to the mainland and the deeper drop off north of it. In the few times that I have fished here during an outgoing tide, I really lucked into the flounder. The main problem with the area is the boat traffic on week ends can sometimes be heavy. Go north to **Roundtable Reef** (See Figure 23 – "A") or to the deeper area in Figure **26 "F" – page C6**. The area between the islands in Figures 23 "C" and **26 "C" – page C6,** is very shallow and I have caught quite a few small reds during very high tides while fishing this area.

Figure 25. Robins Park at Smith Point.

2. Smith Point: End of Road 562. Directions: Instead of turning on Hawkin's Camp Road, stay on 562 until it ends, which is only about two blocks past the Camp Road. This will put you at the confluence of **East Bay** and **Trinity Bay**. The shoreline bottom is mainly sand and there are a lot of pilings around which flounder will usually hang out and about 25 yards north, there is recently replanted sea grass that rat reds love. The shoreline in both the north and south direction is great for wading. This is not a place I would launch a kayak because there is a two or three foot concrete barrier at the water's edge and it is hard to get the kayak out of the water. (See Figure 27)

Figure 27. Smith Point, end of Hwy. 562.

3. The western most end of East Bay (north shoreline) can be reached by going to Smith Point. **About 100 yards before you get to Hawkins Camp Road, the road maintenance will end and there will be a sign for Smith Point Baptist Church on the left side. This is Plummer Camp Road** and just like the other two areas at Smith Point, this is a great place to fish by either wading or by launching a kayak because of all the structure close by: sea grass, oyster reefs, and pier pilings. One very productive reef in the area is **Sheldon Reef.** (See Figure 23 "B")

Another area to fish is the south side of the southern most island (**Willie's Head**) where there is slightly deeper water. (See Figures 23 "D" and **26 "D" – page C6**) To the southwest of this island there are numerous large reefs all the way to Eagle Point across the bay. It is my understanding that at one time, during the early historyof Texas, herds of cattle were walked/swam across the bay between Smith's Point and Eagle Point. This was, of course, before the ship channel was built and before industry and towns pumped so much water out of the ground that the land subsided.

4. Marinas and Bait Shops: Jay Woody's Bait Camp. 409-355-2308. Live bait. The only bait camp in the area. **Turn left on Plummers Camp Road and it is the second house on the left.**

Please Note: At the time of this rewriting, an extensive system of geotubes is being laid out around Robins Park, susposedly for the purpose of preventing silt from being deposited in the channels I discussed in this section. When finished, the fishing in this area should be even better.

TRINITY BAY

East Shoreline, Anahuac

1. See Smith Point.

2. Fort Anahuac Park. Directions: (See Figure 28) **Take I-10 east to exit 810 (Anahuac and Hwy 563 exit). Take a right on 563 and after 6 miles you will intersect Hwy. 61 where you will turn right**

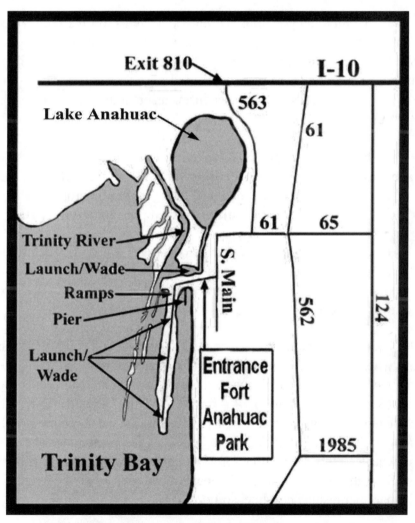

Figure 28. Fort Anahuac Park. Not drawn to scale.

and go 0.7 miles to South Main in Anahuac. Turn left on South Main and in 1.0 mile you will see a sign at the entrance to Fort Anahuac Park on the right. After entering the park, take the fork to the left to go to the boat launch and lighted pier. Restrooms are located in a small unmarked building before you get to the pier.

It does not matter if you are wade fishing or launching a kayak, there are a lot of options:

    a. First, as you approach the boat ramps, on the north side, there is a slough that has easy access for wading or launching a kayak, but does not get very much attention from anglers. This area is shallow and there may be more patches of mud here than in the bay, but it should hold both reds and flounder during an outgoing tide. (See Figure **31 "A" – page C7**).

    b. There are two boat launches: one on the left (east) side launches into the cove between the mainland and the fort peninsula and one on the right (west) that will take you to numerous cuts and sloughs, and to where the **Trinity River** empties into **Trinity Bay**.

    c. At times I have seen a lot of mullet a short distance from the ramp. Look for a trail that goes over a foot bridge on the west side boat launch; you can follow this trail and use your cast net from shore or from the bridge.

    d. The park peninsula extends for 1.6 miles and you can **launch anywhere along this shoreline on the east side** and fish the wide channel between the peninsula and the mainland that leads out to the bay (See Figures 29 and **31 B" – page C7**). This is a good area to fish if the family is tagging along for a picnic, because the shoreline is well kept by the park and it is easy to keep an eye on the kids. The one drawback to this area is that on weekends there can be a lot of boat traffic in this channel. There is a boat cut that runs down the length of the park peninsula shoreline, so I don't recommend wading.

Figure 29. Fort Anahuac Park, East Side.

    e. Another option would be to **launch or wade out about half way down the park peninsula on the west side and paddle straight out to the islands, which are about 300-400 yards out** (See Figures 30 and **31 "C" – page C7).** There is very little boat traffic here and the bottom is mainly sand with shallow patches of mud, plus sea grass along the shoreline. If you paddle north and stay between the peninsula and the islands, it gets very shallow and this area will at times hold redfish and flounder. I would fish the points of the islands and the channels between the islands when the current is moving. **Paddle through the cut between the two islands and then go NW to the mouth of the Trinity River**, which is about 400 to 450 yards away. Fish around the small islands at the mouth of the river. Do not try to wade to the islands on the west side of the Trinity River because the channel gets deep in places, just on the other side of the nearest islands. This area can hold decent water when the wind is blowing hard out of the north, east, or southeast. The only really bad time to fish around Fort Anahuac Park is after there has been heavy rain north of Houston and the Trinity River is dumping a lot of freshwater into the bay or when the wind is out of the south or southwest.

Figure 30. Fort Anahuac Park, West Side.

f. Driving to the end of the long peninsula, you can wade to the south or west to fish Trinity Bay. The bottom is mainly sand and shell with patches of soft mud. There are a lot more options if you have a kayak. **Paddle out SW of the end of the peninsula into an area that is called the Anahuac Pocket** where you will probably see several boats drift fishing. In addition, there are a lot of grass shorelines and sloughs up and down the Trinity Bay east shoreline that can be fished.

g. There is an excellent lighted pier just before you get to the boat launch. I have never tried it, but the pier is in an excellent location for night fishing as long as there is not a lot of boat traffic. (See Figures 28 and **31 – page C7**)

h. The **Lazy Pelican Bait Shop** is the only place to buy shrimp for fishing the north/eastern side of Trinity Bay or Lake Anahuac. **It is located on Hwy. 563. 409-267-4601.**

North Trinity Bay

Small Marsh Lake: Cotton Lake

There is a public ramp on Cotton Lake, which is a small, shallow body of water above the HL&P Cooling Pond. **Directions: On I-10, take exit 565 and turn south. Turn right when you come to 3246 (on some maps this is Gou Hole Rd.) and follow this road through several turns to the ramp.** Paddle across to the other side of the lake and there are a lot of sloughs, cuts, and islands to explore and fish around. I went on a sightseeing" tour of this area so I haven't actually fished here, however the water looks brackish and it probably holds bass as well as redfish.

West Trinity Bay

McCollum Park

Directions: (See Figure 33). **If you are coming from I-10, take Exit 800 and turn right on Hwy. 3180. After about three or four miles, 3180 will merge with 2354. Continue straight and you will be on 2354. It is about three more miles to McCollum Park Road. The only way you can turn is left. If you are coming from south of Baytown, go over the Fred Hartman Bridge in Baytown (Hwy. 146). Stay in the right lane and take the 146 business route after leaving the bridge. It is 2.6 miles from the base of the bridge to Spur 55 (Fisher Drive); this turnoff is not well marked. Turn right onto Fisher Drive and in 6.8 miles, Fisher Drive will dead end on TriCity Beach Road (hwy. 2354). Turn left and in 1.1 miles you will turn right onto McCollum Park Road; this road is also not well marked. The park will be 1.3 miles on the right and there is not a sign marking the park.** Take the trail down a rather steep slope to the water. (See Figure 32) The bay here is hard sand with a thin layer of mud on top and you can wade or paddle all the way to the **HL&P outlet canal** (on the left, or north, about ¼ mile) or to **Point**

Barrow on the right, or south. The HL&P outlet canal is a known producer of trout in cooler weather and if you are lucky, you may catch one of the striped bass the Texas Parks and Wildlife have stocked. Anyone that wades this area needs to be careful of the discharge area because the water gets deeper.

Figure 32. McCollum Park. Looking Down at Shoreline.

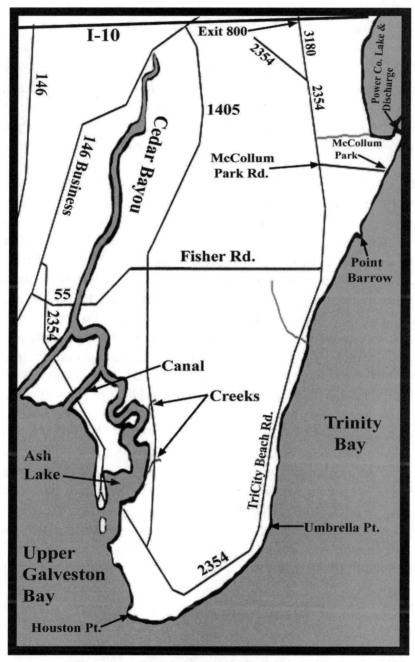

Figure 33. Cedar Bayou & McCollum Park.
Not Drawn to Scale

NORTH (UPPER) GALVESTON BAY

Baytown

1. There is a small park, 0.6 miles from the end of the Fred Hartman Bridge in Baytown (Business 146) (start your odometer at the water's edge). It is on the right side of the road, with easy access. There is a boat ramp, but a kayak could be launched anywhere from the shoreline. I have never thought of this as a wading area.

2. Canal from Cedar Bayou to North Galveston Bay. Directions: (See Figures 33 and 36). Go over the Fred Hartman Bridge in Baytown (Hwy. 146). Stay in the right lane and take the 146 business route after getting off the bridge. About 2.6 miles from the base of the bridge you will turn right onto Spur 55 (Fisher Drive); this turn off is not well marked. TriCity Beach Road (western most part of 2354) is 0.5 miles from 146. Turn right and in about 1.5 miles you will come to a wide canal with steep banks. If you are coming from I-10, there are three options. One route is to take Business 146 (going south) from I-10 and continue to Spur 55, and turn east (left). Once on Spur 55, follow the above directions. A second route from I-10 would be to take Business 146 to Hwy. 1405 and turn left or south. When 1405 intersects Fisher Rd. (Spur 55), turn left (west). This will take you to the western most part of 2354. Turn left (south) on 2354 to get to the canal. A third route that might be better for someone who lives east of Baytown, would be to get on Hwy. 2354 as if you were going to McCollum Park and follow 2354 to Fisher Rd. where you will turn east (left). Stay on Fisher Rd. until you get to the western most section of 2354 and turn left. Note: Hwy. 2354 is not continuous all the way around, because the bridge that crossed Ash Lake (the mouth of Cedar Bayou) was removed some time ago.

This is one of the harder places to fish by kayak because the banks are steep and the water is about 40-50 feet below the bridge. About 150 yards to the right or west is upper Galveston Bay (See Figure 34) and about 300 yards to the east is Cedar Bayou.

At various times, I have seen quite a few of the local people park and fish from the bank. One of the better areas to try during an outgoing tide, would be the point where the canal opens up into the bay. You can expect to catch reds and flounder in this canal along with black drum and sheepshead. I also would not be surprised if a bass or catfish was caught after heavy rains.

Figure 34. Canal: Looking West Toward Galveston Bay.

3. Cove on Ash Lake. There is a great place to launch a kayak that is **slightly further down 2354 (2.8 miles from Hwy. 55).** (See Figures 35 and **37 – page C8). On the left side (east) of the road, there is a cove that enters Ash Lake.** This body of water is to the north of where Cedar Bayou enters Upper Galveston Bay. The cove shoreline has a lot of mud and it is very shallow, however this area, along with **Ash Lake**, is an unspoiled, scenic area and it holds a lot of potential for reds, black drum and flounder. I have often seen families fishing from the shore.

Figure 35. Cove on Ash Lake.

4. The northern most part of TriCity Beach Road dead ends at Ash Lake, where Cedar Bayou joins Upper Galveston Bay. (See Figures 36 and **37 – page C8**) At one time there was a bridge going across Ashe Lake, but it was removed a few years ago. A kayak can be launched at the end of the road, behind the road barrier or you can fish from the shore. There is a lot of mud around the shoreline. **TriCity Beach Rd. will have a fork to the right about 100 yards before it ends and this fork will take you to Thompson's Marina.** If you put in at the marina, paddle north to fish a lot of pilings or go south to the mouth of Cedar Bayou. A little further south will you will find Houston Point and **Dow Reef.**

5. There is a very good launch site on the south side of the mouth of Cedar Bayou; this is where the southern portion of 2354 dead ends and it is also where Crawleys Bait Camp is located. Houston Point is about a 1 1/2 mile paddle to the left, or south. (See Figures 36 and **37 – page C8**).

44

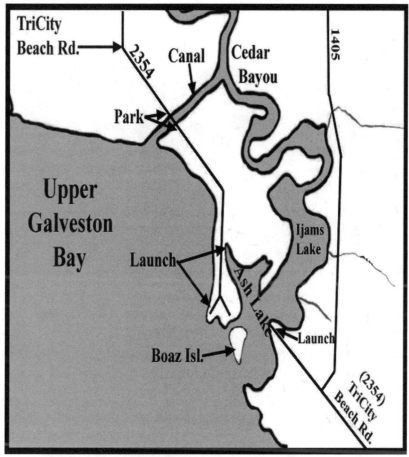

Figure 36. Cedar Oak Bayou. (Not Drawn to Scale.)

6. There are two creeks on hwy. 1405 that allow you to launch into different parts of the lower end of Cedar Bayou; this is not a good place to wade unless you do not mind mud. **The first** (See Figures **37 – page C8** and 38) **creek is 1.7 miles from hwy. 55 and it enters a large cove off of Cedar Bayou. The second creek is called Ijams Creek and it is 3.2 miles from Spur 55.**

The paddling distance to the Cedar Bayou cove is only about 20-30 yards; if you want seclusion and absence of other boaters, then you can not get much better than this.

45

Figure 38. First Small Creek on So. 2354.

7. Baytown Nature Center (Upper Galveston Bay). Directions: It does not matter whether you are coming from I-10 or Hwy. 146, turn onto Decker Drive (Spur 330) and look for Bayway Drive. This road is 1.3 miles from I-10 (turn right) and 3.6 miles from 146 (turn left). Go 1.3 miles and turn right on Shreck road; there will be a sign that says Great Texas Coastal Birding Trail. Stay on Shreck and it will enter the Baytown Nature Center and it ends at a small pier, 1.6 miles from the turnoff from Bayway. There are numerous places to wade or to launch a kayak. One place to start if you are looking for shallow water reds is in a protected area on the right, just as you enter the Nature Center, or 0.7 mile from the Bayway turnoff. It was here where I ran into a Texas Parks and Wildlife trucks that was dumping 100,000 trout fingerling into the bay, and that sold me on the place.

8. Marinas and Bait Camps:

     a. Crawley's Bait Camp. 281-383-3665. Boat ramp, live bait.

     b. Thompson's Fishing Camp. 281-427-2300. Boat ramp, live bait.

MID-GALVESTON BAY AREAS
WEST SHORELINE

Sylvan Beach Area (LaPorte)

1. Barbour's Cut. This place is good for bank fishing or launching a kayak but it is difficult to wade because of a lot of rocks underwater. By kayak, you can paddle south to fish the Upper Galveston Bay shoreline. **Directions: one or two exits north of the LaPorte exit, take the Barbour's Cut Rd. exit and turn right. Turn right onto South Jamison Road and after it curves to the left, it becomes Ballister Road, which will dead end at the launch area.** (See Figures 39 and 42)

Figure 39. Barbour's Cut.

2. Sylvan Beach. Directions: (See Figure 42) **Take 146 to the city of LaPorte and turn east onto Fairmont Parkway. Go 1 mile and the road will almost dead end at Sylvan Beach. You can go straight to the main entrance, or turn left to go to the pier or turn right to go to the boat launch.** It is rather hard to launch a kayak from the shore, because of the rocks in the water (See Figure 40) and there is a barrier at water level, 15 feet from shore in some places. There are a lot of old pier pilings north of Sylvan Beach and south of the ramp is an excellent reef to fish called **Yacht Club Reef**.

Figure 40. Sylvan Beach.

3. The **Sylvan Beach Pier** charges $3.00 for adults and $1.50 for children and seniors. **Linda's Bait Camp is located right by the pier.** 281-471-5705.

4. Upper Taylor Lake. (See Figures 41 and 42) **Directions:** This part of Taylor Lake is between Bay Area Blvd. and Hwy. 146. **Turn onto Port Road from either of the roads mentioned.** There is not a ramp in this area but the banks are well kept and it is easy to launch a kayak from the gentle sloping shoreline. The photo in Figure 41 shows a small creek along Port Road that feeds into the main part of (upper) Taylor Lake. I have not fished this area but friends of mine have caught reds here. I have seen crab traps in the water but other than my friends, I have never seen anyone fish this area.

Figure 41. Creek leading into Upper Taylor Lake.

5. Ramp on Mid Taylor Lake. (See Figures 42 and 43) **Directions: Take Bay Area Blvd. to Red Bluff and turn east and you will come to a bridge in 1.7 miles. An alternate route would be to take Hwy. 146 and turn north on Red Bluff and travel 2.6 miles to the bridge,** the only good place to launch a kayak is on the south side of the bridge where a ramp is located. I have not waded any of the areas around Taylor Lake so I can not describe the bottom conditions.

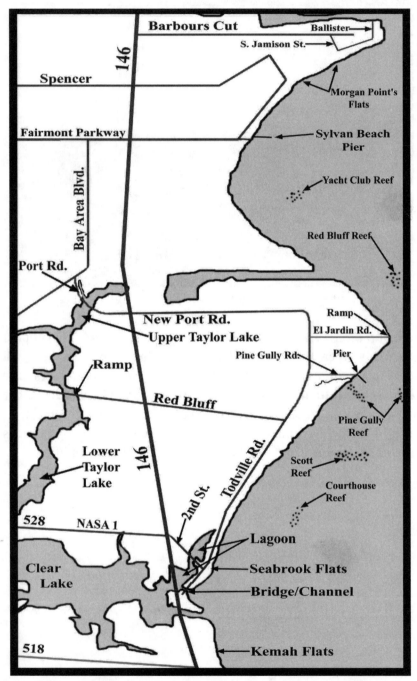

Figure 42. Barbour's Cut to Kemah. Not Drawn to Scale

Figure 43. Ramp on Mid Taylor Lake.

Seabrook Area

1. El Jardin Ramp. (See Figures 42 and 44). **Directions: El Jardin is 1.2 miles from where Red Bluff intersects Todville Road; once on El Jardin, it is a short distance to Galveston Bay.** There is a ramp on the right and an old pier that should hold flounder and sheepshead around the pilings. North of the ramp is **Red Bluff Reef.**

2. Pine Gully Park and Pier. Directions: (See Figure 42) **NASA Rd. 1 turns into 2nd St. in Seabrook and this road dead ends on Todville Road. Turn left on Todville Road and it is 2.5 miles to the park. An alternate route would be to take Red Bluff Road and it also dead ends on Todville Road. Turn left and it is 0.7 miles to the Pine Gully Road and another 0.6 miles to El Jardin Rd.** This is a private park, but nonresidents may pay $4.00 per car to use it. The park is open from 6:00 a.m. to 8:00 p.m. (sunup to sundown). If there is not anyone on duty, look for a drop box near the entrance; put your money in an envelope that is furnished by the park and leave it in the drop box.

There are shell reefs on the north side of the pier and on the south side of the creek that weaves through the park. One to two hundred yards out from a long unlighted pier, there is a large oyster reef that occasionally has some outstanding fishing around it. This is one of the few piers that I don't like because the shore has such a gentle slope; two thirds of the pier is in very shallow water. Walk out to the end of the pier and fish the small reefs that are on both sides of it. I have not waded this area, however the shore appears to be mainly sand. It is a short paddle from the El Jardin ramp to the **Pine Gully Reef** and this is a good alternate put in if you are planning to fish this area.

Figure 44. El Jardin Ramp.

3. Seabrook Lagoon and Flats. (See Figure 42). There are a couple of places, north of the Kemah boat channel and below Hwy. 146 bridge in Seabrook where you can go crabbing, wade fishing or launch a kayak. **Directions: Take NASA Rd. 1 to Hwy. 146. Cross over 146 and NASA Rd. 1 turns into 2nd Street. Right before 2nd Street intersects Toddville Road there is a great place to go crabbing.** The city of Seabrook has built a very nice park on the bridge that crosses a small body of water that I call "the lagoon" and it is perfect for families to picnic and crab or fish. Sidewalks line the water on both sides of the street and there are benches to sit on while you fish or watch your kids.

Turn right on Toddville Rd. and you will come to a low bridge, where a kayak can be launched or where you can wade the flats in the bay or the small lagoon on the other side of the bridge. The best place to park if you are wading depends upon which side of the channel that you want to fish. The channel may be as much as twenty feet deep if there have been recent storms in the area. The city has provided a black topped parking lot on the north side of the bridge, however, if you plan to wade the south side of the channel, then park next to a small bird observation platform, which is behind the pink Maribelles. Fish the bay side of the channel on an outgoing tide and the lagoon side on an incoming tide. (See Figure 45 and 46). I have seen people wading the lagoon, but I have never tried it. An alternate put in point would be under the 146 bridge; there are boat ramps and other places to launch on both sides of the bridge.

If you are wading the bay side, be very careful of the broken pilings and concrete that can lie hidden under water. Over time, these become encrusted with barnacles and oysters and they are razor sharp. In cooler weather, fish the piers from a kayak. Large trout will hang close to the pilings, seeking heat from the sunlight hitting the piers.

4. Kemah Flats, Landry's Restaurant. (See Figure 41) **Behind this Seabrook restaurant, about 35-50 yards from shore,** there are broken concrete blocks underwater where a lot of redfish are sometimes found. A wader can enter the water about 50-70 yards south of the restaurant and just north of the some old piers that line the shoreline. Another place to enter the water is from 8th street in

53

Figure 45. Bridge on Todville Rd., looking south.

Figure 46. Bridge on Todville Rd., looking north.

Kemah. Live bait can be purchased at the 3 Amigo's Bait Camp in the Seabrook Shipyard which is on the other side of 146 at the base of the bridge.

San Leon Area

1. Small Boat Ramp. (See Figure 47). **Take Hwy. 646 from the Gulf Freeway (I-45) and go east. You will cross Hwys. 3 and 146. Go straight for 40 yards past the second yellow blinking light at the end of 646 and follow the road to the left (north) past Clifton's By The Sea** (a good seafood restaurant). **About 50 yards down on the right is a ramp** that is great for either launching your kayak or for entering the water to wade. I have never used this ramp, but I have seen cars and trailers parked on either the upslope or down slope of the ramp. There are a lot of pilings in the water to fish around and several oyster reefs in the area.

2. San Leon Reef. This reef is down the shoreline, north of Eagle Point Marina. It is between two piers: One at HL&P outlet and the other at 18th street. The best way to fish this reef is by kayak. It is hard but not impossible to wade out from or to launch a kayak at HL&P outlet because of the submerged rocks. Probably **a better place to get into the water is at 26th Street which is 1.7 miles from the blinking yellow light.** Go to the end of the street and park in front of the end of the road warning barrier; there is a vacant lot to the right of the barrier where you will be parking. (See Figure 47)

3. Todd's Dump, Red Fish Reef (Bar) and Red Fish Island. There is a very large oyster reef extending out southeast from Eagle Point Marina and it ends about thirty yards from the south end of Red Fish Island. (See Figure 47) This area is very productive during a rising or falling tide, unless the oyster boats are actively working the reef, which does not occur during the summer. This area should only be fished from a kayak; the surrounding water is too deep to wade. Even in a kayak, be careful of cargo ships going down the ship channel for at times they can throw up three foot waves that have been known to swamp unsuspecting power boaters. About eight years ago, a wader was washed off the reef by one of these waves and subsequently drown.

There are two places where I usually launch my kayak if I plan to fish around Red Fish Reef. One option is to go to Eagle Point Marina, however this is a very popular spot for power boaters and at the present, they do not cater to kayaks. Another option is to go a short distance down East Bayshore Drive to San Leon Marina and use their ramp. A third option, and the one I prefer, is to launch at Factory Bayou. (See#2, page 58)

I have not fished here since **Red Fish Island** was destroyed by storms, but I am sure it will again prove to be one of the better places in Galveston Bay to fish. Note: Todd's Dump is an old name that you do not find on all of the new maps.

West end of Red Fish Reef/Bar: 29.488 N, -94.874 W

4. April Fool Flats and April Fool Reef. This reef is between Eagle Point and April Fool Point. You can exit 646 from I-45 and follow it all the way to the bay. After crossing 146, you will turn right at the second blinking yellow light and the road becomes Bayshore Drive. This blinking yellow light is 7.5 miles from I-45. Follow Bayshore Drive for 3.5 miles and it will end on Hwy. 517. Turn right on 517 and in 0.3 miles, 517 will turn right again at a blinking red light. To get to April Fools Reef, turn left onto Ave. I at the blinking red light and it will dead end at the reef. After parking, you will have to walk down a slope to get to the water. If you followed Bayshore Drive to the end, Eagle Point Marina would be on the left. You can launch a kayak from Ave. I, or if you do not want to carry it up and down the slope, use Eagle Point Marina. I have only fished this area in a kayak and from the shore so I can't say anything about the wading conditions. (See Figure 47)

5. Piers: (See Figure 47).

    a. Bayside Park & Spillway Pier. 281-559-2403. **This pier is exactly one mile from the yellow blinking light.** They sell fresh dead bait and there are restrooms and a grill. Open 24 hours a day.

    b. The HL&P spillway is in between the Bayside Spillway Pier and Bayshore Park. This park has a narrow wooden platform that parallels most of the spillway. Fish from this platform or launch a kayak along the rocky shoreline. If you are wading, you should enter the water at the far south shoreline so that you will be away from the current and any holes around the spillway. There are also rocks in the water and this makes it difficult to wade.

    c. 18th Street Pier. 281-339-2600. **This pier is exactly three miles from the blinking yellow light.** They are open 24 hours and there are restrooms and a grill; call in advance to check on the availability of live bait.

Dickinson Bay

1. There is a very good and little used **boat ramp under the overpass on hwy. 146** on the north side of **Dickinson Bayou**. **Dickinson Bay** is to the left (east). The shoreline has numerous reefs and pilings that are productive, however I probably spend most of my time in the middle of this bay fishing **Dickinson Bay Reef**. (See Figures 47 and **48 – page C9**)

    I have never been to the west however I have seen reports of occasional catches of redfish and flounder from this area. I have been told that there is an abandoned marina to the west on the south shoreline that has deeper water around the piers and pilings; this would probably be worthwhile checking out.

2. If you are interested in fishing the north part of Dickinson Bay, then launch your kayak on a small stream called **Factory Bayou**. This is a good way to fish **April Fool Point** and **April Fool Reef**. **Take 517 through the city of Dickinson and continue to the bay. About 100-200 yards before the last traffic light, you will cross a small bridge over an inlet from the bay or if you are coming down Bayshore Drive from 646, turn right onto 517. The road will turn right and you will come to the bridge mentioned above. Park by the bridge and there is an easy launch into the water and it is only a short distance to Dickinson Bay.** There is a large reef, starting just south of April Fool Point and extending half way to the mainland that is excellent to fish **(Dickinson Reef)** however there are times that boat traffic can be heavy in the area. (See Figures 47 and **48 – page C9**)

3. Marinas and Bait Camps.

> **a. Eagle Point Marina.** 281-339-1131. Boat ramp, live bait.

> **b. San Leon Marina.** 281-339-1515. Boat ramp, live bait.

> **c. Spillway Bait and Tackle.** 281-339-0486. Live bait.

> **d. 3 Amigo's.** 281-474-7447. Live bait.

> **e. T. C.'s Bait camp**. 281-559-1231.

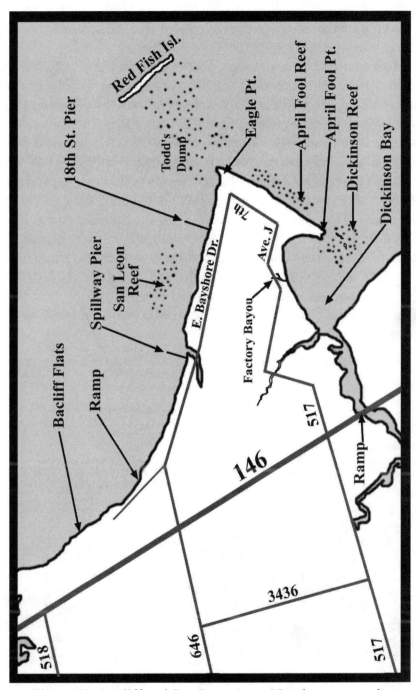

Figure 47. Bacliff and San Leon Area. Not drawn to scale.

Texas City Area

1. Moses Lake. Moses Lake and **Dollar Bay** are best fished from a kayak or from the shoreline. There are two deep holes in Moses Lake that can hold fish in the heat of summer or the cold of winter. One hole is right inside the flood gate and the other one, which is deeper, is found in the northwest corner. I have not had as much luck fishing the hole near the gate, probably because this area has the swiftest water flow, making it difficult for fish to stay in the area. (See Figure 49) Normally when I am in my kayak, I will start out fishing the marsh area south of the gate, which can hold reds and flounder during very high tides or I will try the shallow shoreline as I am paddling toward the northwest corner. It is also a good idea to work the bulkheads and salt grass areas around the homes that are found along the south shoreline. Another area to try if the boat traffic is light, is the shoal islands and the channel that leads from Moses Bayou to the flood gate.

Figure 49. Moses Lake at the Flood Gate.

2. Launch Sites At Moses Lake:

a. **There is a place to launch a kayak into Moses Lake at the Flood Gate.** (See Figures 50 and 55) **Drive to the end of the Levee road and on the left you should see a small slough or cut** that goes out into Moses Lake from the canal that parallels the **Levee Road**. The only problem is that you must take the kayak down the slope of the levee to reach it; the hard part is dragging the kayak back up the slope after fishing all day.

Figure 50. Channel To Moses Lake at Flood Gate.

b. **There is another way to get into Moses Lake from the Levee Road** that I like better than the one by the Flood Gate. **Look on the left side of the road (going toward the Flood Gate), immediately after the stop sign and the large building on the left and you will see a canal** that feeds water from Moses Lake to the **pump station**. The bank is not as steep and thus it is a lot easier to launch a kayak. (See Figures 51 and 55)

61

Figure 51. Channel To Moses Lake at Pump Station.

c. The best way to get to Moses Lake by kayak is by launching at the far west end. (See Figures 52 and 55) **Take 1764 from I-45 to Texas City and turn left (north) on 146. Drive exactly 1.7 miles and you should come to a crossover to the south bound side of 146 immediately before going over Moses Bayou. Turn left onto the crossover and then turn right onto the elevated grass area to park.** Launch your kayak and go to the right to get to Moses Lake; it is impossible to go to the left because of a very low railroad bridge.

d. An excellent way to get to all areas of Moses Lake is to launch at one of the marinas. **Directions to the marinas**: (Easy Way) **From I-45, take Exit 16 to Hwy. 1764 (same as Emmett F. Lowry Expressway). Continue on 1764 past Hwy. 146 into Texas City; 1764 becomes Palmer Ave. Turn left on 23rd St. and go all the way down to 36th Ave. where you will turn right. Go three blocks on 36th Ave. and turn left on 20th St. Ray's Bait Camp and Marina is about a half mile down on the left.** It is an easy paddle from the marina to almost any part of Moses Lake.

3. Moses Bayou. (See Figures 52 and 55) If you want to go to a place that boaters can not get to but is easy for anyone with a kayak, then this is for you. The only time I have seen anyone fishing here, they were on the railroad bridge. The west end of Moses Lake narrows down to Moses Bayou and it crosses under Hwy. 146. On the east side of 146 going north, is the Texas City Prairie Preserve. Boaters can not get into this area because there is a very low railroad bridge that crosses the bayou and completely blocks it off. In fact, a kayak can not get under it since it is so low to the water. **Directions: If you get on Hwy. 146 by turning left off of 1764 (go north on 146), drive exactly 2.1 miles to the crossover immediately after the bridge/overpass. Crossover to 146 southbound and look for a shell road on the right just before the bridge. Turn right onto this shell**

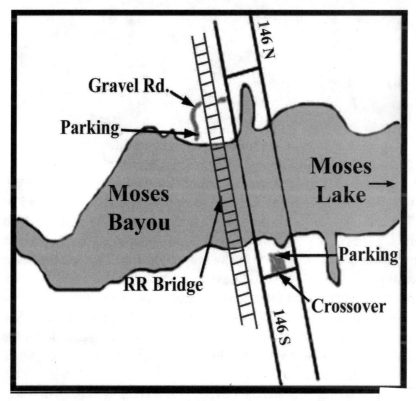

Figure 52. Moses Bayou. Not drawn to scale.

road which will go over railroad tracks; park next to the water to launch a kayak. There are approximately 2-3 acres of water with several sloughs leading off from the bayou. The main channel narrows, but you can follow it for miles. This area is difficult to wade because the bottom is mainly mud. Fish here only on an outgoing tide; I would suggest adding about 45 minutes to the tide time for the Flood Gate.

Figure 53. Texas City Levee Rd.

4. Texas City Levee Road. (See Figures 55 and **58 – page C10**) **Directions to the Texas City Dike and Levee Rd.: Exit I-45 at 1764 and stay on it all the way through Texas City until it dead ends.** Turn right, go one block to the light and turn left. To get onto the **Levee Road, turn left at the stop sign at the top of the levee leading to the Dike.** Once past the 20 mph sign, you can park anywhere on the right to go wade fishing. Look on the pavement for the painted white dashed lines; this indicates the parking area. (See Figure 53) There will probably be cars parked all up and down the road and you will see waders fishing 50-100 yards from shore. Once parked, you will have to walk down a long grassy slope to get to the water. The shoreline along the Levee Road is shallow enough to wade, with most of the area having a hard sand bottom. There is also a special area reserved for sail boarders about two miles down and the fishing is restricted here.

5. The Gazebo. Along the levee there is a large gazebo and in front of this gazebo there is a deep hole that will sometimes hold fish.

6. Dollar Point and Dollar Reef. Dollar Point is 2.2 miles down the Levee Road where the road bends to the left (west). The reef is very large and it starts close to the shore. Dollar Point Marina is located at the base of the reef and they have a pier if you do not want to wade. **Dollar Flats** extends along the entire shoreline of the levee, up to Dollar Point. **Levee Flats and Levee Reef** extend from Dollar Point to the flood gate. If you have a kayak, launch at Dollar Point Marina and it will save you from having to pull the kayak up and down the hill. Night fishing under lights can be tremendous, especially if the tide is moving. (See Figure 55)

7. Half Moon Shoal is about half way down the levee before you get to sail boarding area. It is about 300 yards from the shoreline and you will probably see boats anchored in a half circle around the shoal. Fish the northeast edge where there is a drop off into water five to seven feet deep. (See Figure 55)

8. Flood Gate. Go to the end of the levee road to get to the flood gate. You can fish from the shoreline next to the Flood Gate or wade the flats before you get there, however do not wade close to the flood gate due to fast currents and deep water. In addition, there are a lot of concrete blocks in the water that make wading difficult. These same currents, during an outgoing or incoming tide, make this a great place to catch flounder. Fish the inside or the west side of the gate on an incoming tide, and fish the outside or east side on an outgoing tide. A lot of people set up lights to fish here at night. (See Figure 54 and 55)

Figure 54. Flood Gate, Bay Side.

9. Bait Camps:

   a. Dollar Point Bait Camp. 409-945-4808. Boat ramp. Live
   bait. Pier.

   b. Bait Camps: Ray's Marina and Bait Camp. 409-945-
   0989. Boat ramp, live bait.

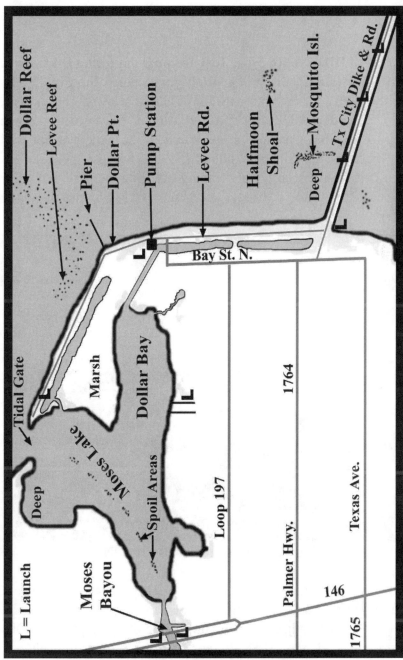

Figure 55. Moses Lake to Texas City Dike
Not Drawn to Scale.

Texas City Dike

1. Base of Dike, South Side. Just as you go onto the Dike, on the south side (right), there is a small park, called the First Ladies Pavilion Park, where you can wade or launch a kayak. There is a reef about 70 yards out, however if you are wading, be careful because the Texas City Ship Channel is just south of the park. Do not wade anywhere else on the south side of the dike because the water gets deep fast. I have seen people wading out from the park, but I have never tried to wade this area. (See Figures 55, 56, and **58 – page C10**)

Figure 56. First Ladies Pavilion Park

2. Mosquito Island, Texas City Dike. This area is great for both walk-in wading and kayaking. Wading can be done at the base and most of the area adjacent to the north side of the Texas City Dike. (See Figures 55, 57, and **58 – page C10**) Be very careful wading the base of the north side because there is a deep hole that lies between the mainland and what is left of Mosquito Island. You can see the

68

shell island, especially during a low tide, 200-300 yards down from the base. Look for anglers wading out along the eastern side of the hole. If there is a high tide and you do not know where to find the east side of the drop off, check your odometer in your car; it is about 0.3 mile from the stop sign at the top of the levee to the spot where you should walk in, give or take ten yards in either direction. Fish the drop off to the west or the shallow side to the east. The bottom on the east is mainly sand and shell with only occasional mud being found. At the base of the "island", there are a lot of small clumps of oyster shell that a person could stumble over.

Figure 57. Mosquito Island.

During the summer, I often drive out onto the dike just to check the water, and I often find the north side calm and clearer than the south side. The north side of the dike is protected from a south and southwest wind and it is somewhat protected form a southeast wind. Once you drive past the Mosquito Island area on the dike, there are many fine places to park and wade or to launch a kayak. If you do not want to wade, there is a pier on the left side, 1.4 miles from the stop sign. Crabbing is also excellent from the shoreline.

Be careful when wading any area around the dike. Large ships going down the ship channel will sometimes suck out a tremendous volume of water from the flats and when it returns, sizeable waves may result. One or two people usually drown here every year. Another cause of concern is the increase in the number of car burglaries that I have read about in the last few years that occurred either on the dike or on the levee. I would think twice about leaving my car parked here at night.

3. Texas City Dike Pier. This pier offers the deepest water adjacent to a pier in the state. This is probably one of the best places to fish for black drum in the Galveston Bay system. **The pier is located at the very end of the Dike.** Open 24 hours. 409-948-8172.

4. Bait Camps:

a. **Anita's Bait, Tackle and Seafood.** 409-945-5727.

b. **Boyd's One Stop.** 409-945-4001.

c. **Curl's Fisherman's Headquarters.** 409-948-3894.

d. **Lee's Bait and Tackle.** 409-945-5675.

e. **50-50 Bait and Tackle.** 409-945-2506

Areas Around The Causeway

Hitchcock Diversionary Canal

Directions: Take Exit 15 (Hitchcock Exit) from I-45. Turn left on 2004 (before you get to the dog track). Turn right at the 1st stop sign, and then a left on hwy. 6. Turn right on 2nd street (2nd light). Go past the Hitchcock Fire Dept. and there should be a parking lot on the left before you get to a bridge. Park here and fish along the bank.

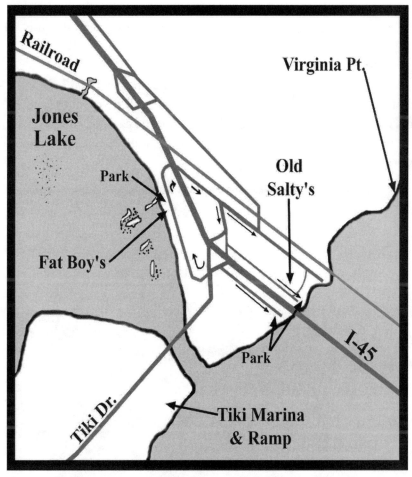

Figure 59. Jones Lake and North End of Causeway.
Not Drawn to Scale.

Jones Lake

1. Beach Area next to Fat Boys and Jones Lake. Directions: Take Exit 4 (Tiki Island exit) and circle back around to the right and Fat Boy's will be on the left just before going under I-45. The sign is usually propped up against the side of the building and is hard to see. Drive as far as you can past Fat Boys to park and it will be easier to launch a kayak or to get to the north shoreline of Jones Lake. A lot of kayakers put in at Fat Boy's and paddle to **North Deer Island**. Another option is to drift the north shoreline and fish the many oyster reefs. There is a very good reef that you should try on the south side of Tiki Island.

Waders will find this is better place to park and it is only a short walk to the North shoreline of Jones Lake. (See Figures 59, 60, and **61 – page C11**) Almost all of the shoreline can be waded; most of the bottom is sand with small pockets of shallow mud, interspersed with rocks and oyster reefs.

Figure 60. Fat Boy's Parking and Shoreline.

2. North Shoreline of Jones Lake. The railroad frowns on this, but having said that, there are a lot of people that go to the north shoreline by walking down the railroad tracks. This is not something I recommend, but if you decide go to the north shoreline this way, please be careful. There is a canal that the railroad track crosses, so when wading this area be careful of drop offs. Even when a person is familiar with an area, recent storm surges may have increased the channel's depth. A short distance from this canal, the shoreline becomes flat and easier to walk. This area of Jones Lake is a great place to fish, whether you are walking the shoreline or wading waist deep.

3. Another place to launch to get to the northwest end of Jones Lake is on Highland Bayou, at Louis bait camp on Hwy 6 and I-45. It is about a fifteen to twenty minute paddle to Jones Lake, but if you hurry through this area, a lot of good fishing will be missed. There is a large marsh that drains into the bayou and the many sloughs and cuts can hold a lot of flounder and red fish. A great float plan is to start at the bait camp and drift with an outgoing tide down to Jones Lake. Fish Jones Lake until the incoming tide starts and then fish the bayou and sloughs in the marsh again while being carried back to the launch ramp. Along the way, you will pass under a low railroad bridge, but unless the tide is extremely high, you shouldn't have any problem. For the waders that don't have a kayak, you can rent a small boat and motor at the bait camp for a very reasonable price. (See Figure **61** – **page C11**)

Once you get to Jones Lake, the mouth of the bayou you just left and another cut or slough to the east of this bayou can have outstanding fishing on an outgoing tide (See Figure **61 "A" and "B"** – **page C11**). I know everyone has their favorite red fish hole and this is one of mine. I have seen a large number of reds in this area at various times during the year. A word of caution to kayakers: the bayou passes by a subdivision and on occasion power boaters will roar out of their canals without looking, as they head to Jones Lake.

North Side of Causeway and Lower Galveston Bay

1. Good areas for launching kayaks at the base of the Causeway. Directions for the northwest end of the Causeway: Exit at Tiki Island (Exit 4) and go straight down the feeder all the way to the water's edge at the base of the Causeway. Drive past the "end of the road barrier" sign to park. (See Figures 59, **61 – page C11** and 62)

Be careful wading under the causeway because there is a lot of rebar and cement chunks around and between the supports; boats have been known to lose their lower units if they weren't careful. You can easily wade to the east toward **Virginia Point**: the bottom is mainly firm sand and there are a lot of scattered oyster reefs and small patches of mud.

Figure 62. NW Side of Causeway

2. An even better place to park is on the opposite side (northeast) of the freeway, a short distance from the old Salty's Bait Camp. This area is larger, with a relatively flat concrete apron on the side of the Causeway. **Directions: Take Exit 4 (Tiki Island exit) and circle back around to the right, past Fat Boy's. Go under I-45 and turn right, toward Galveston; this will take you to the water's edge.** (See Figures 59, **61 – page C11**, 63, and 64)

Figure 63. NE Side of Causeway, Parking.

Launching at either place is a great way to get to get to North Deer Island or to fish the north shoreline of West Bay. There are a lot of small and medium sized rocks around the immediate shoreline; the largest being about the size of a football helmet.

3. Oyster reef at Virginia Point. Launch your kayak at the old Salty's Bait Camp under the Causeway and paddle to the east around Virginia Point by going under the railroad bridge. There is an oyster reef just off of Virginia Point. Do not drive under the railroad bridge to get closer to Virginia Point because this is private property.

75

Figure 64. NE Side of Causeway, View of RR Bridge.

South Side of Causeway and Lower Galveston Bay

1. Directions for the south end of the Causeway. You will find a very large, nice parking area on the southeast (Galveston) side of the Causeway. This is on the east side of I-45; the Galveston Bait and Tackle Camp is on the west side. **Directions: Heading south on I-45, go over the Causeway and exit at the Harborside/Teichman Rd. Turn left at the stop sign and go under I-45. Turn left onto the feeder road, after the last building on the right, and just before you enter I-45, you will make a small jog to the right. Go behind the railing and turn onto a gravel road, which will end at the base of the Causeway.** (See Figures 65 and 67)

I enjoy paddling out to fish the railroad bridge when it is hot in the summer. At times I find a lot of fish under the arches of the bridge, especially when the tide is moving. If the tide is coming in, either position yourself on the east side of the RR bridge and let the current

76

carry your soft plastic lure or live shrimp under the arches, or get on the other side of the bridge and cast up under the arch and let the current carry it back out. If the tide is going out, use the opposite strategy. The fish are using the RR arch as an ambush point and it also probably offers some shade.

Do not overlook going under the causeway and paddling to the west to fish the shoreline around Galveston Bait and Tackle. There are numerous reefs in the area that are seldom fished. Most of the power boaters that launch at the ramp of the bait shop are in a hurry to get to greener pastures, not realizing that they are passing up some great red fishing. You can also launch a kayak at the bait shop, just stay out of the way of the power boaters.

Figure 65. Southeast Side of Causeway.

2. The west side of the south causeway has a ramp at the bait stand that is very popular with boaters, however you will have to pay a small fee for using it. I don't recommend launching from this area on the week end. There is a shell road that parallels the causeway road on this same side (west) which is lined with rocks that is very popular with people who fish from the bank. (See Figures 66 and 67) You can park anywhere along the road and fish from the rocks. I have not tried wading this area, so I can not give any information on the bottom or the water depth.

Figure 66. Shell Rd. on Southwest Side of Causeway.

3. Marina's and Bait Camps:

a. **Galveston Bait and Tackle.** 409-740-1185. Boat ramp. Live bait.

b. **Fat Boys.** 409-935-4151. Live bait, boat ramp.

c. **Louis Bait Camp.** 409-935-9050. **(Hwy. 6, across bridge from Bayou Vista)** Boat ramp, live bait. (Galveston Bay Boat Rentals) Rents small 14 foot flat bottom plywood boats with 15 hp outboards.

78

d. Smitty's. 409-744-7705. (71st Exit) Live bait.

e. The Baiten Place. 409-744-9152. (61st Exit) Live bait.

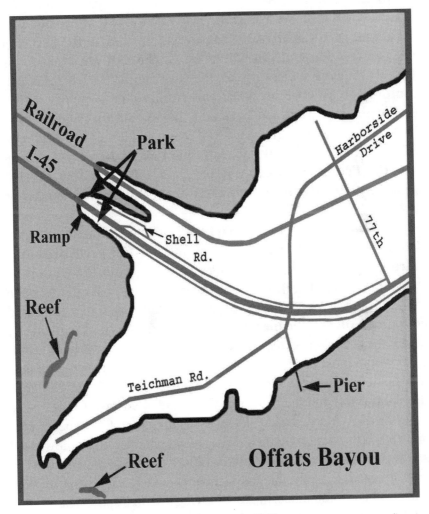

Figure 67. South End of Causeway.
Not drawn to scale.

Galveston Island

Sea Wolf Park

1. Directions. (Most Direct Route) **Stay on I-45 into Galveston and turn left on 51st Street.** This road will take you to Sea Wolf Park. A shorter route with less traffic would be to **exit at Harborside/ Teichman, once you cross the causeway. Turn left at the first stop sign you come to and you will be on Harborside Dr.** This road is also a shortcut that will take you to the Strand and to the ferry crossing. **Continue on Harborside until you come to an overpass with a light at the top. Turn left here and this should be Pelican Road** (turn right and you would be on 51st Street and it will take you back to I-45 in town). **After taking a left onto Pelican Road, you will go over the Pelican Causeway Bridge, past Texas A&M Marine University, and here the road's name changes to Seawolf Parkway.**

THE BEST PLACE **to park and fish or to launch a kayak, is to turn left down a dirt road about 100-150 yards from the entrance to Sea Wolf Park (about 2.5 miles from the end of the Pelican Island Bridge).** This is a public road and it has tall brush and trees on both sides of the entrance. **Turn left down this road and continue until you see the water on the right;** this puts you directly across the "cove" from the pier and the park and about 400-500 yards from where most people enter the water to wade. You can park next to a small beach unless there has been a lot of rain. Waders can go to the right or left and the bottom is firm sand. **Caution**: I have fished this area a lot (both on a kayak and by wading) and I have never seen any wakes thrown up by the ferries or by container boats, however I am aware that several people have reported on the internet that this has happened. Actually, this can occur anywhere along the ship channel whenever large container ships are moving at a high speed. (See Figure 69 – page C12)

If this road is muddy, you have two options. Some people park on the paved road about 100-200 yards before the entrance to Seawolf Park, however a word of caution: there are "no parking"

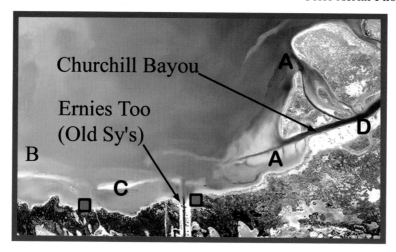

Figure 1. 2002 Aerial Color IR Digital
Image from Texas GLO.

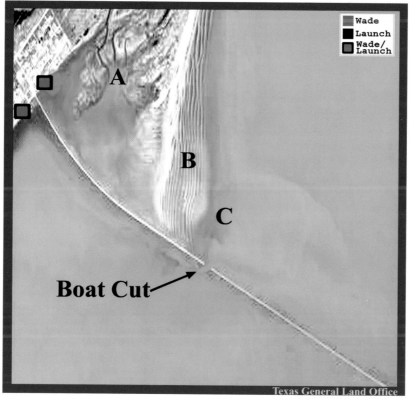

Figure 14. North Jetty, Bolivar.

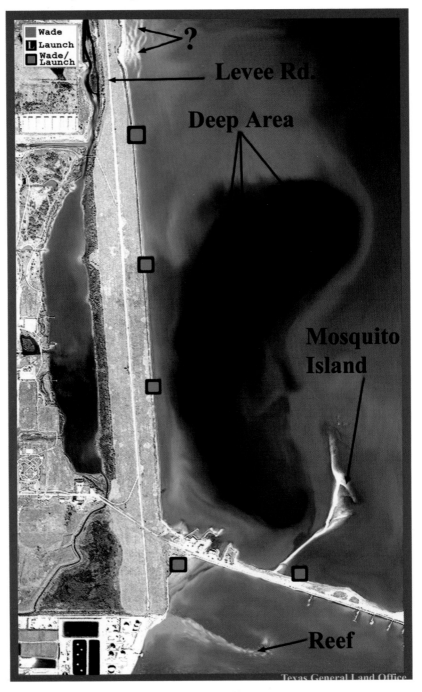

Figure 8. Bolivar.

Figure 15. North Jetty, Bolivar.

Figure 100. SLP: Looking Toward Follets Isl.
Photo by Curley Myers.

Figure 17. Rollover Pass.

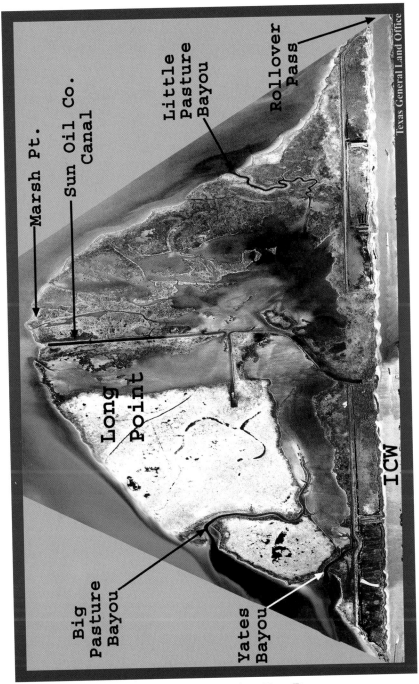

Figure 22. Marsh Point, East Bay.

Figure 26. Smith's Point.

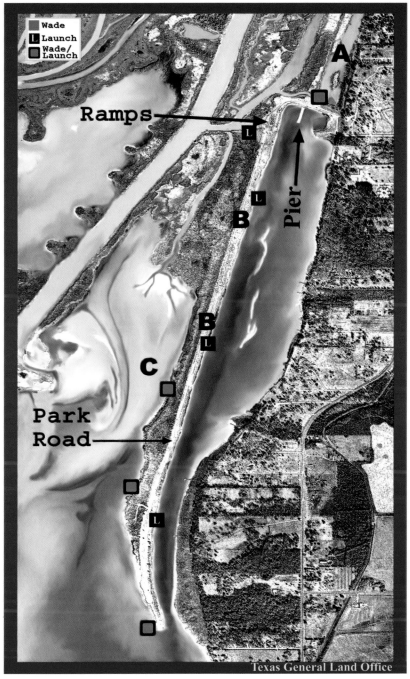

Figure 31. Fort Anahuac

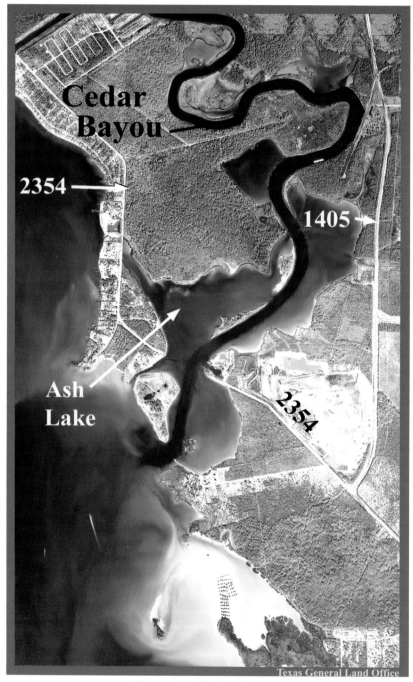

Figure 37. Cedar Bayou

Figure 48. Dickinson Bay.

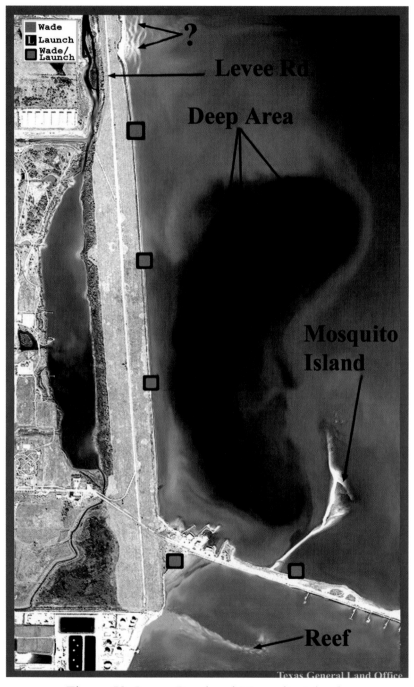

Figure 58. Levee Road and Mosquito Island.

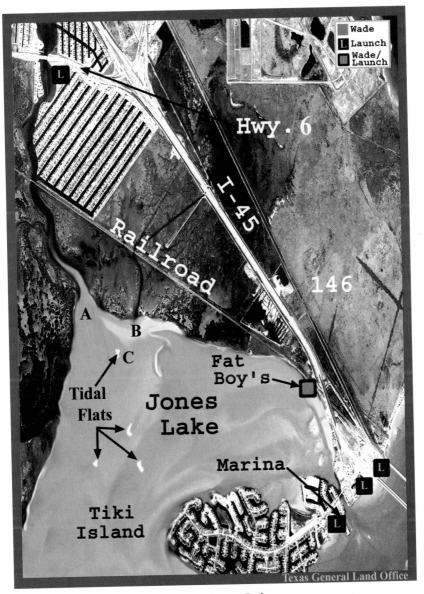

Figure 61. Jones Lake.

Figure 69. Sea Wolf Park.

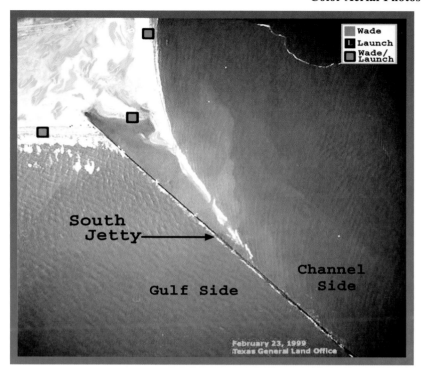

Figure 71. Galveston South Jetty.

Figure 101. SLP: Brazoria County Park.
Photo by Curley Myers.

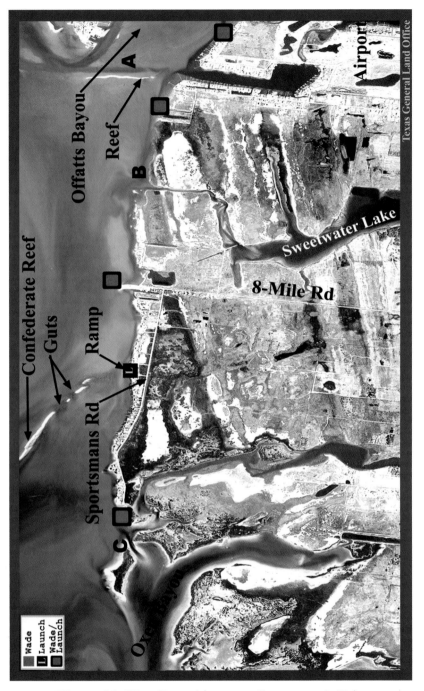

Figure 86. West Bay: Airport to Sportsman's Rd.

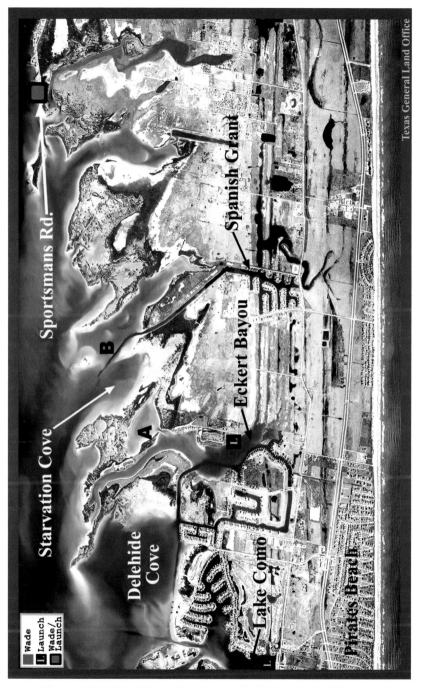

Figure 92. West Bay: Sportsman's Rd to Lake Como.

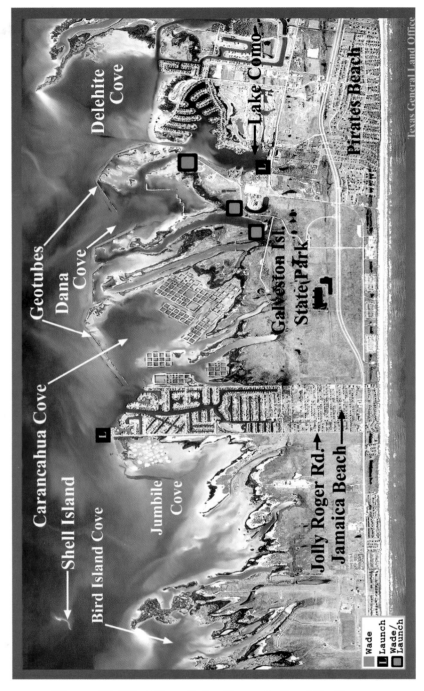

Figure 93. West Bay: Lake Como to Jumbile Cove.

C16

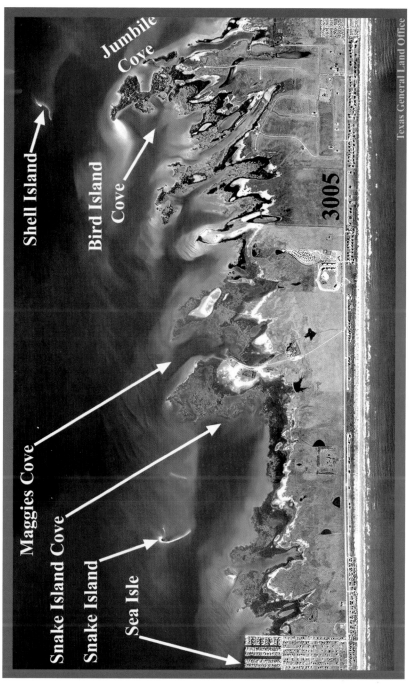

Figure 96. West Bay: Jumbile Cove to Sea Isle.

C17

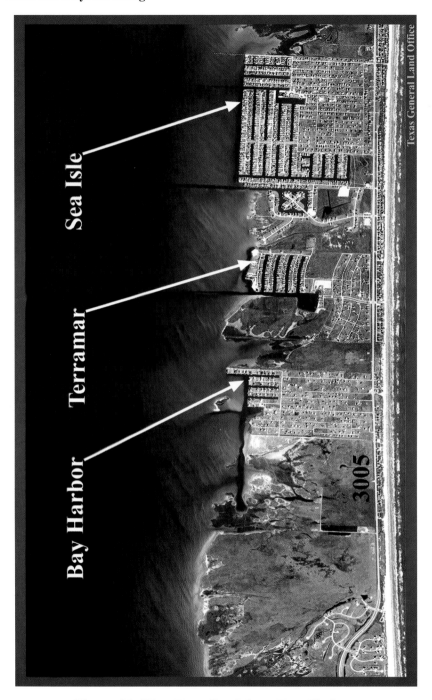

Figure 97. West Bay: Sea Isle to Bay Harbor.

Figure 98. West Bay: Far West End.

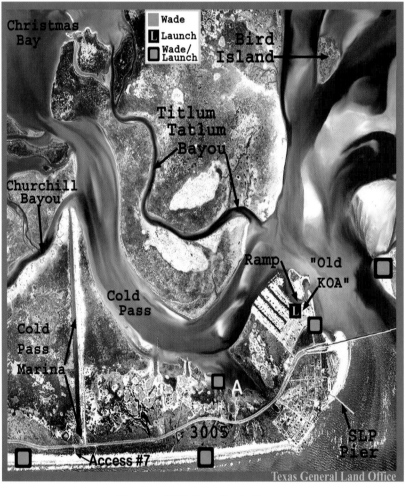

Figure 104. San Luis Pass.

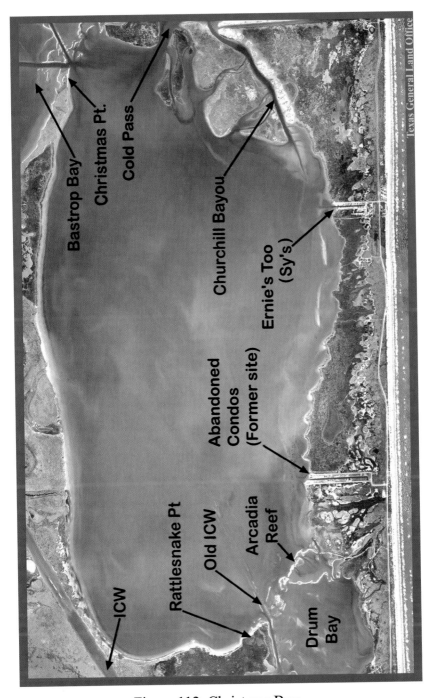

Figure 112. Christmas Bay.

Figure 113. Christmas Bay, East End.

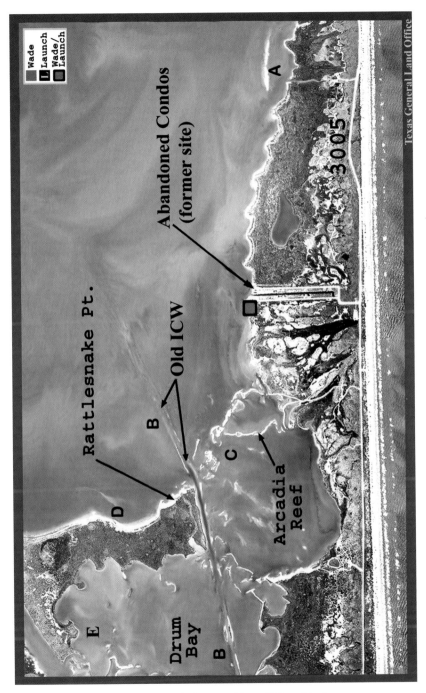

Figure 114. Christmas Bay, West End.

Figure 118. Drum Bay.

signs posted along the road, and occasionally the cars parked in this area are towed away. (See Figure 68) If you do park here, it is only a short walk to the water, and an angler can wade fish on either the north or south side of the road. The other option is to pay and go into the park itself. The park is open from sunup to sundown, but there is someone manning the parking lot 24 hours a day during the summer and it costs $5.00 a car to park. **(409-744-5738)** Other than Rollover Pass, I would say that Seawolf Park is probably the most popular place to fish for flounder in the fall.

Figure 68. Alternate Parking. (not recommended)

The water on the right (south) borders a boat channel and you can only wade out about 50 yards. There are a lot of rocks and other junk on the bottom so be careful wading. The area on the left (north side) is where most people fish because the footing is firm and you can wade out a long way, however, as you go north and get out of the "cove", the amount of mud increases and it gets more difficult to wade. Another option is to fish from the rocks that are found all around

81

the island; a lot of bull reds are caught on the east and south sides from these rocks because the park is at the confluence of the Galveston Ship Channel and the Houston Ship Channel.

Kayakers have more options with the concrete ship a short paddle to the north and all of the small guts along the shoreline north of the park. Most of the guts are unusual in that they run perpendicular to the shore instead of parallel to it. This is also a great place to rig a rod behind the seat and troll with a soft plastic lure, however be sure to hold on, for a lot of large fish can be found in the area due to the ship channel being adjacent to it. (See Figure **69 – page C12**)

Concrete Ship: 29.344 N, -94.786 W

2. Seawolf Park Pier. Sea Wolf Park has a pier that is very popular, especially in the fall diring the flounder run. The pier is open 24 hours a day in the summer and in the fall, it is open all night on Friday and Saturday only. It costs $3.00 for adults and $2.00 for kids under 12. The best place on the pier to fish is close to the rocks, right next to the shore.

3. ***If you want **to wade fish the bridge area, there is very limited parking on the left just as you cross the bridge to Pelican Island, right in front of tall posts. Park here and walk** back toward the bridge and down the slope to the water. Wade back to the right (north) to fish. There is room for two or three cars at the most.

Galveston South Jetty

1. Directions: Drive east, to the end of the Seawall Blvd. Turn right on Boddeker Dr. which will take you to **R. A. Apffel Park.** Parking is $5.00. I often arrive before they start collecting fees and no one seems to worry about the fishermen, in fact, I have offered to pay on the way out but have been refused every time.

2. Channel Side. This area has become very shallow and there are sand bars exposed most of the way down this side of the jetty. Not long ago, the channel side was lined with bait camps along with several launch ramps. One good thing that has resulted from the channel side being shallow is that it allows someone to walk out a long way before having to get onto the rocks. Usually every summer there is a growth of slippery algae and most veteran rock walkers have taken their share of slips and falls. If you insist on walking on the rocks, it would be wise to invest in a pair of cheap golf shoes: the cleats will help with the traction.

The flats on the channel side have a lot of fishing potential since there are shallow areas next to very deep water (the ship channel). You should think of this as being a place to try not only in summer but also in the fall and winter. In the cooler months, the shallow flats and the rocks warm up fast and many fish go into this and similar areas in the bay to feed. This area can also be a good place to catch bait that hold close to the rocks. Be careful and wear a pfd since tankers will at times create large waves as mentioned in an earlier section, that may knock a person off the rocks or wash them into a deep area.(See Figures 70 and **71 – page C13**)

3. Galveston Pocket. The base of the South Jetty on the Gulf side is protected from strong east or NE winds. Most people fish this area from the rocks; I do not usually see people wading. However, if a you can find a time when the water is somewhat clear, the waves are small and the rocks are not crowded, wade fishing can be outstanding on a moving tide. (See Figure **71 – page C13** and 72)

The general rule of thumb is to fish the channel side on an outgoing tide and the Gulf side on an incoming tide.

Figure 70. South Jetty, Channel Side.

Figure 72. South Jetty, Gulf Side.

84

4. The Lagoon. Actually there are two lagoons now.

   a. The New Lagoon. The body of water on the east side of Boddeker Dr. is fairly new. It was built to create more wetlands and to give a better outlet for "The Old Lagoon" which is found on the west side of the road. This newer lagoon is small and shallow, however there are walkways built along the shoreline in various places and this makes it a nice place to take the family crabbing and fishing.(See Figure 73 and 74)

Figure 73. New Lagoon.

b. The Original Lagoon is long and perhaps three to five feet deep in most places. (See Figure 75 and 76). **You can park and enter the water just past Nash's Lagoon Bait Camp, which is on the right just as you turn off of the Seawall Blvd. onto Boddeker Dr. (409-763-9069).** The water can be very swift close to the bridge on an incoming or outgoing tide, however it is a great place to fish for flounder and reds. In addition, I can remember newspaper posts in the past, stating that a surprising number of large specs have been caught here.

85

Figure 74. New Lagoon, Further North.

Figure 75. Lagoon: View From Boddeker Dr.,
Looking West.

86

Figure 76. Lagoon: View From Seawall.

5. Marina's and Bait Shops:

a. **Basin Bait Camp.** 409-762-3168. (Galveston Yacht Basin) Boat ramp, live bait.

b. **Nash's Bait Camp.** 409-763-9069. (Just off Seawall Blvd. at S. Jetty) Live bait.

Galveston Seawall Beachfront

1. East End of Seawall Blvd. The Seawall Blvd. dead ends at the east end of Galveston, at the Galveston Ship Channel, a couple of miles north of the south jetties. Park by the road barrier and follow a path over large rocks, down a slope to the water. (See Figure 77) At the water's edge there are several unique and different places to fish. One hundred yards north, there are large granite rocks lining the shore that help prevent erosion. About 50-75 yards out, there is a hole 20-30 feet deep. (See Figure 78) This area can hold fish during summer and winter, plus it is a great place to catch bull reds. South of these rocks and for most of the way to the south jetties, the beach is shallow and it can be easily waded. (See Figure 79) **Please be aware that with the ship channel as close as it is, there are occasionally 2-4 foot waves that are sometimes generated by passing boats.**

An additional danger is the undertow that is generated when the water is initially sucked out by the boats propellers. This undertow can be extremely strong as evidenced by several young girls on vacation that drown in this area a couple of years ago. Be sure to wear a PFD. Also to the south, behind the beach, there is a canal that drains a large area of water that is called "the lagoon". Most of the canal is very shallow but it has a lot of structure that can attract reds and flounder during high tides. The shoreline is easy to walk and sightcast to fish, however, most of the time I don't give it a second thought unless there is a very high incoming or outgoing tide. (See Figure 74)

Figure 77. East End of Seawall, Parking.

Figure 78. East End of Seawall,
Looking North.

Figure 79. East End of Seawall Blvd. Looking South.

2. Rock Groins. The small jetty structures (rock groins) were originally put in place to try to stop beach erosion, and even though the plan failed, they became extremely successful fish holding structures. There are four of these to the east of the Flagship Hotel about 0.1 mile apart and ten to the west of the hotel that are somewhat closer together. A few of these are very short but most extend out at least to where the 2nd sand bar would be found. (See Figure 80) One thing I have noticed while viewing the aerial photos from different sources, is that the guts that parallel the beach are not as prominent between the rock groins as they are in other areas. (See Figure 82) This lack of bottom structure makes it even more important to key on the area close to the rocks, especially if you are looking for flounder.

Figure 80. Rock Groins along Seawall.

90

A fishing technique you might keep in mind if it is a slow day, is to get as close to the water as possible, in the middle of the rocks leading out to the end, so that you can cast both toward the shore and toward the deeper end. Cast a small, soft lure (or live bait) parallel to the rocks edge and drag or hop the lure slowly back. Gradually fan your casts out away from the rocks and be sure to throw in both directions. The rocks of the groins do not extend out as far as they do on the Surfside jetties, so with a little practice, you will be able to judge where the rock edges are located. I have caught a lot of flounder doing this, especially when the tide is moving.

3. Flat Rocks at Seawall Blvd. Waters Edge. Turn right onto Galveston Seawall Blvd. from 61st Street. This is a stretch of beach that was not restored with sand and the water comes right up to rocks which were laid so they made a somewhat flat walking surface. The water averages two to three feet deep at the edge of the rocks. Twenty five to thirty feet further out is a sand bar, which is about where the second bar would occur. (See Figures 81 and 82)

Figure 81. Flat Rocks Along Seawall.

Figure 82. Flat Rocks Along Seawall.

This is an area that I fish when I don't have a lot of time but I feel that I have to run down to the coast to wet a line or go crazy. The flat rocks make it real easy to walk and cast, almost like walking the rocky shoreline of a lake. (See Figure 81) Flounder, reds, specs and sheepshead cruise the gut next to the rocks so make sure you cast parallel and right next to the rocks. The only time I avoid this area is when there is a large influx of sea weed from the gulf during spring and early summer.

***For all of the people who fish for sharks and bull reds, and who wade out to the 1st or 2nd bar to cast, this is the place to go.** You are closer to deep water: On the rocks, you are standing almost on the 2nd bar without having to wade. (See Figure 82) When the surf is extremely rough, I have seen people stand on the steps to cast.

4. Rock Pile Out in Surf? There is a pile of rocks 100-150 yards from the shore **almost directly in front of the I HOP Restaurant** along the Seawall. This is a location I got from a very old Joe Doggett column, in the Houston Chronicle (15 years ago?). I haven't fished here or tried to locate the rocks but if they exist, it definitely would be a place that could attract a lot of fish and no one else would know about it.

5. West End of Seawall. The end of the seawall has some deep guts due to unusual currents caused by the seawall. This is a hard place to fish because there are almost always people swimming or playing in the surf along this stretch of beach.

6. Piers:

    a. Flagship Fishing Pier. 409-763-8696.

    b. Galveston Fishing Pier. 409-744-2273. (Located at 91st St.) This pier is closer to deep water than the 61st pier.

    c. 61st Street Pier. 409-744-8365.

Beach access between seawall and San Luis Pass

Since beach access by nonproperty owners is under scrutiny by the Galveston city council, the access roads listed below may change at any time.

0.5 miles from seawall (17.7 miles from SLP): Pocket Park #1

1.2 miles from seawall (17.0 miles from SLP)

2.2 miles from seawall (16.0 miles from SLP) – Pocket Park #2

2.8 miles from seawall (15.4 miles form SLP) – Hershey Beach

3.2 miles from seawall (15 miles from SLP) – Parking close to beach

3.6 miles from seawall (14.6 miles from SLP)

4.35 miles from seawall (13.85 miles from SLP) – Pocket Park #3

6.1 miles from seawall (12.1 miles from SLP) – next to Pirates Beach

6.4 miles from seawall (11.8 miles from SLP) – Galveston St. Park

7.6 miles from seawall (10.6 miles from SLP)

7.8 miles from seawall (10.4 miles from SLP) – Jamaica Beach

8.6 miles from seawall (9.6 miles from SLP)

10.0 miles from seawall (8.2 miles from SLP)

11.2 miles from seawall (7 miles from SLP) – Parking close to beach

12.2 miles from seawall (6 miles from SLP) – Parking close to beach

12.7 miles from seawall (5.5 miles from SLP)

13.1 miles from seawall (5.1 miles from SLP) – Parking close to beach

13.6 miles from seawall (4.6 miles from SLP)

14.5 miles from seawall (3.7 miles from SLP) – Parking close to beach

14.6 miles from seawall (3.6 miles from SLP)

15.8 miles from seawall (2.4 miles from SLP) – Point San Louis

Offats Bayou

1. North South Shoreline. There are not any legal places to park and enter the water on the north shoreline of Offats Bayou. The best way to fish area is by kayak launched from the south shoreline or from the park on the south end of the Bayou, along 61st Street.

2. South Shoreline. There are **two great access points near the airport and the entrance of Offats Bayou;** while they are close together, they can take you to quite different fishing structure.

    a. There is an area just north of the Galveston Airport that allows a kayaker easy access to some of the deeper holes of Offats

Bayou, the north shoreline, and several large reefs near the mouth of the bayou. (See Figures 83 and 85) The grass shoreline is shallow however a wader should be careful of unexpected deep drop offs; be sure to wear a pfd. Notice the boat cut on the east side of the reef that is in the middle of the entrance to Offats Bayou. (See Figure **86 "A"** **– page C14**) **Directions: Turn right on Stewart Road from 61st St., and follow it all the way to the airport. Once past the airport, there will be a golf course sign on the right and you will turn right on the next street (99th St.). Follow this road until it dead ends on Air Way Lane, and turn right. Air Way Lane will end at a small clearing where you can park.**

Figure 83. Adjacent to Airport.

b. About 50-75 yards west of the above site is an area that does not have as much room for parking, but **there is a small, gravel boat launch. The directions are basically the same: Turn right on Stewart Road from 61st St., and follow it all the way to the airport. Once past the airport, there will be a golf course sign on the right**

and you will turn right on the next street (99th St.). Here the directions differ: **After a very short distance, you will turn left onto Schaper Rd. and then make a right on 103rd St.; follow this road to the bay (about 0.5 mile).** (See Figures 84 and **86 – page C14**)

To the left of the launch (west), there are several small coves, reefs, islands, and sloughs that could hold decent fish. A short distance from the launch, you will see a long narrow canal/cove that is somewhat shallow, but when the tide is ebbing, the fishing can be great for flounder and redfish. Five hundred yards NE of the boat launch, at the entrance of Offats Bayou, you will find the large oyster reef mentioned above and it is plainly visible at low tide. Launching at the above two sites will allow a person to fish not only Offats Bayou but also the western most part of West Bay.

Figure 84. Launch at 103rd St., Looking at Causeway.

c. Pier on Offats Bayou, north shoreline. Directions: Take the first exit (Harborside/Teichman Rd.) after getting off the

97

causeway in Galveston, and turn right at the stop sign. This road dead ends at the pier entrance. They are not always open so it is best to call first. **409-740-9990.**

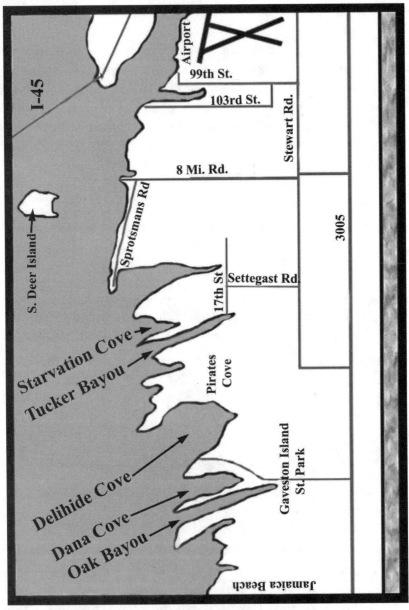

Figure 85. West Bay: East End. Not drawn to scale.

West Bay To Brazos River

West Bay

1. Sportsman's Road. Directions: (See Figure 85) **Go south on Sea Wall Blvd. and shortly after it ends and turns into San Luis Road, turn right at the first blinking light and this will be 8-mile road. It is four miles from 61st St. to 8-mile road. It is another two miles to Sportsman's Road and the only way you can turn is left. Half way down 8-Mile Road, you will have to take a small jog to the left where it crosses Stewart Road. There is a public boat ramp between two houses 0.8 miles from the turn. It is 1.3 miles to the end of Sportsman's Rd. where there is a small parking area** and this is where most people wade or launch their kayaks. (See Figure 87)

Figure 87. Sportsman's Rd. Parking, Looking West.

There are many coves, sloughs and islands to fish south and west of the area where everyone parks. One of these is a cut between a small island just west of the end of the road and a point on the

99

shoreline. During the fall, both sides of this cut have yielded flounder when the tide was moving. Fish the east side of the cut before crossing over to the small island. Behind the parking area, the water is shallower and at times I have seen a lot of rat reds along the back shoreline. (See Figure 88)

Another name for Sportsman's Road is **Anderson Ways**.

Figure 88. Sportsman's Rd., Looking SW.

Confederate Reef is a large oyster reef that parallels Sportsman's Rd. and extends almost out to **South Deer Island**. The main part of the reef is usually visible during a low tide, however there is a lot of deep mud that you have to wade through to get there. The reef has three cuts just off the south shoreline, about halfway down Sportsman's Road; the southern most gut is rather deep. You can easily cover the distance out to South Deer Island in a kayak, and if you have a fishfinder you should be able to locate the guts which show up real well on the aerial photo in Figure **86 – page C14**. In the summer, this area is heavily fished and it usually has a lot of power boat traffic.

2. End of 8-Mile Road. Drive to the end of 8-mile road (0.1 mile past the turn off to Sportsman's Rd.). There is a large parking area and a bait camp on a small peninsula at the end of the road. (See Figures 85, 89, and 90) This is a location where I have the best luck in the fall or spring. Do not wade on the left or west side where there is a boat cut. There are a lot of rocks in the parking area and in the water close to shore. You will find a lot of mud to wade through and about 200 yards to the east, are there several rusted out barges. The outlet to **Sweetwater Lake** (See Figure **86 "B" – page C14**) is in this same area, and it can be a great place to fish on an outgoing tide. **J. W's. Bait Camp** is located at the end of 8-mile road. **(409-737-3457)**

Figure 89. 8-Mile Rd. Parking.

Figure 90. Rusting Barge East of 8-Mile Rd.

3. Small Boat Ramp on Eckert Bayou (Tucker Bayou). (See Figure 91) **Turn left on 8-mile Rd. and after 0.3 mile, turn left on Stewart Road. Go 2.7 miles and turn right on Settegast. This road will curve to the left and after 0.8 miles it will end at a boat ramp** that is across from Lafitte's Cove Subdivision. I have not waded the canal shoreline for many years so I can not comment on the bottom, but this is a great place to launch a kayak. There are many days when it is too windy to kayak the bays, but Eckert Bayou seems to be somewhat protected. Fish the canal for reds or flounder or go around to the right and fish **Starvation Cove.** This is one of the few ways to reach this cove by kayak. During very high tides, it is sometimes possible to paddle across a mash area to reach to reach it but if the tide goes out, be prepared to paddle back the long way or to drag your kayak across a lot of mud. The paddle through this area during a high tide can offer a lot good fishing to the person looking for redfish or flounder. (See Figure **92 "A" – page C15**) Keep in mind that Starvation Cove historically has yielded more nine and ten pound trout than any other area in the Galveston Bay System. In addition, it has yielded three state record flounder and one state record sheepshead. Located on the east side of Starvation Cove is a deep channel that comes from the Spanish Grant subdivision. The west side has very soft mud and is hard to wade. Fish this area not only when there are tide changes, but also during the heat of summer. Another option is to paddle east and fish **Delehide Cove.**

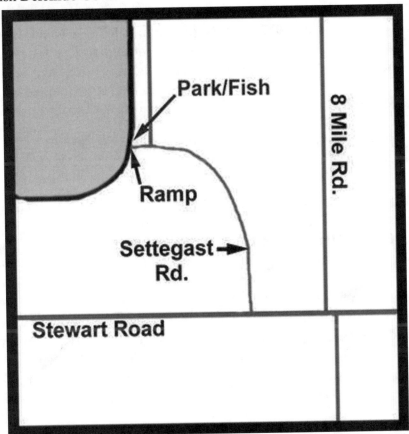

Figure 91. Boat ramp on Eckert (Tucker) Bayou.

4. An excellent place to launch a kayak if you are going to **Delehide Cove** or **Dana Cove** is **Pirates Beach Marina. Directions: Stay on Seawall Blvd. until you come to 13 Mile Road. Take a right on this road and then a left at the first stop sign. When you get to the**

Pirates Beach subdivision, look for the marina. Some people will put in on the west side of the parking lot, on the shore of Lake Como, instead of launching at the marina. Paddle north through Como Lake and turn left at the first cut or slough you come to. This cut is where I caught my personal best largest flounder plus numerous reds. (See Figures **92 "A" – page C15** and **93 – page C16**)

5. Galveston Island State Park. Directions: (See Figure 85) **Traveling west on 3005, or Termini – San Luis Pass Road, turn left or south toward the beach, to sign in and to pay for your vehicle;** if you plan to fish here a lot, buy the yearly pass, the Texas Conservation Passport. The pass will also help you get into the park early in the morning when the gate may be locked. Usually a person can call ahead and get the combination to the lock if they have the yearly pass; in any event, it doesn't hurt to try. Go back to the stoplight and cross the main road to get to the bay.

Once you enter the park, there are several places to launch a kayak or to start wading: **(1) turn left at the first road after entering the park and within a short distance you should see the end of Oak Bayou**; you will have to drag your kayak about ten yards. This is not the best place to enter the water, in my opinion, but I have waded here in the past, before I bought a kayak. The bottom is firm sand and the water is about waist deep. **Instead of turning left, (2) stay on the road that entered the park and a short way down this road there is a small clearing or boat launch on the left on Oak Bayou.** The best option, **(3) stay on this main road all the way to the bay.**The shore has mud about a foot thick, but further out, the bottom becomes mainly sand.

There are a lot of coves and bayous that can be fished from a kayak or waded. The cove you will be launching into is **Dana Cove**. This area has changed so much in the last couple of years, I hardly know it anymore. Texas Parks and Wildlife has set up GeoTube barriers to act as a breakwater and to protect areas in the back of the cove where they have replanted sea grass that once grew throughout the

104

bay system. (See Figures **93 – page C16** and 94) In addition, they have dredged out eight to eleven foot deep channels on the bay side of the tubes to use in the back of **Carancahua Cove** to make what looks like small growing plots of the sea grass in a checkerboard appearance. There are two reefs located in the mouth of this cove. What all of this amounts to, is a lot of structure that is perfect to fish from a kayak. **Carancahua Reef** is about a mile paddle to the NW. This is a large oyster reef situated 7 to 10 miles west of the causeway that runs north and south, and just about divides West Bay into two parts. At low tide, you can easily see the middle part of the reef.

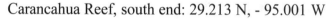

Carancahua Reef, south end: 29.213 N, - 95.001 W

Figure 94. GeoTubes in State Park.

6. Jamaica Beach. (See Figure **93 – page C17**) **There is a ramp in Jamaica Beach off Jolly Roger Road that allows easy access to Carancahua Reef, although you have to paddle approximately 0.5 miles through canals to get to the bay. Directions: From 3005,**

turn onto **Bob Smith Dr. in Jamaica Beach and then turn right on Jolly Rodger Rd. Make a left on Destin Rd. and the ramp will be on the left.**

Another place to launch or wade, is on the east side of Jamaica Beach: **continue following Jolly Roger Rd. even after it turns left and parallels the state park. Watch for Barbados Way, which will dead end on Jolly Roger.** Pull over to the right and park on the grass and there will be a narrow, short sandy beach where a kayak could be launched into a slough on the west side of Galveston Island State Park. Fishing options include paddling east to **Carancahua Cove** or west, to **Jumbile Cove.** Northwest of Jumbile Cove are the **Shell Islands** and **Bird Island Cove.**

Bird Island: 29.179 N, -95.024 W

Shell Island Point: 29.185 N, -95.014 W

Shell Island: 29.191 N, -95.013 W

7. Sea Isle. This area has a special place in my heart because many decades ago, I had my first West Bay wade fishing experience around the coves close to Sea Isle. It as also here that I saw my first redfish, rooting around on the bottom along those same shorelines. **Snake Island Cove, Snake Island**, and **Maggies Cove** have excellent fishing potential. The best way of reaching this area is by **launching your kayak at West Bay Marina in Sea Isle.** (See Figures 95 and **96 – page C17**)

All of this area has an excellent sand bottom for wading, unless you get into some of the marsh areas along the shoreline. Snake Island is a shell island that is shaped like a quarter moon and it is always visible except under extremely high tides. It is slightly deeper on the north end, on the inside of the curve and on the south end, a short distance out. I have had good luck walking the island shoreline and casting to both sides. Pay close attention to the ends of the island,

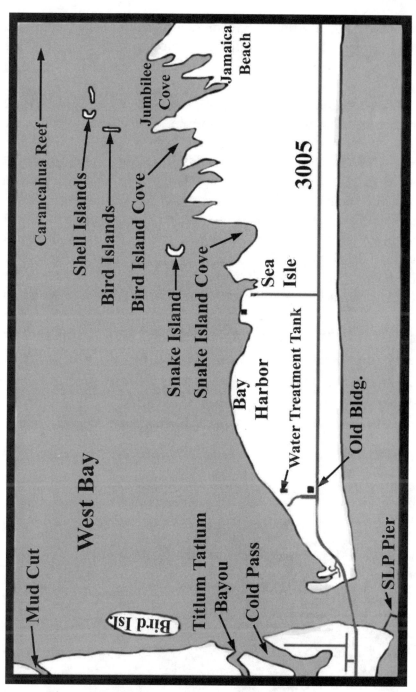

Figure 95. West Bay: West End. Not drawn to scale.

especially when the tide is moving. A turbulence is set up in this area and flounder will often be waiting to ambush baitfish. I lost a flounder of a lifetime a few years ago while fishing the points.

8. Far West End. The shoreline from **Sea Isle to San Luis Pass** not have as many coves, however this does not mean the area is featureless. Look at the shallow areas in Figures 95, **97 – page C18** and **98 – page C19**, and notice the rippling effects in the sand. The average angler, and that included me many years ago, may not realize what the bottom contours look like in this part of the bay, since the shoreline does not have the coves and sloughs that are found just a mile or so northeast of here. I admit I have waded this area many times and enjoyed the fishing without understanding why the fish were there. The bottom structure, plus the close proximity of San Luis Pass, makes this a great place to fish.

Please note that any of the areas discussed in this section may be closed to future fishermen. At the time of printing, the city of Galveston was debating what access rights to grant to nonproperty owners.

Figure 99. West Bay: Old Water Treatment Plant.

rights to grant to people who like to drive up to a fishing location and get out to wade and fish or launch a kayak.

     a. There is a gut behind the toll booth on the Galveston bay side of the San Luis Pass Bridge, about 150 yards out. A popular place to park to access this area is what is called the "old water treatment plant". **Look for a small, rundown building on the north side of 3005 and an old water treatment tank closer to the water, 0.6 mile before you get to the toll bridge.** (See Figure 99) **Turn right on a paved road that ends after 20 yards and then continues as a dirt road leading back to the bay** (See Figure **98 "B"** – **pageC19**) There is space for five to seven cars to park. Wade out NW from the shore on a hard sand bottom and continue until the water starts getting deeper; you will be at the edge of the first gut. There is a second gut about 200-300 yards further out. These channels (guts) are outstanding places to fish if the tide is moving. Specs will cruise around the deeper guts and wait for baitfish to be washed over the edge of the gut.

     b. Another option is to drive to the toll bridge on the Galveston side and exit either to the right on the sand/gravel road next to the bridge. (See Figures **98 "A"** – page C19) **Look for a dirt road on your immediate right. Take this road to a small canal** where you can either launch a kayak or have an easy wade out into West Bay/San Luis Pass. Once past the area around the canal, the bottom is hard sand and you can wade a long way and not get over waist deep, as long as you stay out of the guts. If you continue straight instead of turning onto this road, you may encounter soft sand so be prepared to get stuck if you do not know the way around this area. On the week ends, there will often be pickups waiting around to pull cars out for a fee. I prefer to exit Hwy. 3005 at Rusty Hook and drive on the beach to San Luis Pass if I decide not to use the canal mentioned above. This is a much slower way to get to the pass but I don't have a four wheel drive vehicle. However, it does have the advantage of allowing me to see several miles of the surf and there have been times when I would change my fishing plans when I saw feeding activity close to shore.

There will probably be people fishing and parking both under the bridge and back around by the bay. Wherever you park, just be sure to be above the high tide line; there have been a lot of sad waders that have returned to find their car submerged to the floorboard or worse. If you decide to use the canal leading into West Bay, never start your wade or launch a kayak without first making a few casts into the canal. There is a lot of mud present and it is not deep, but twice in the many times I have put in here, I spooked several large red fish.

10. Surf around San Luis Pass, Galveston Side.

a. On the Galveston side of SLP there is a **major trough between the 2nd and 3rd sandbar**. This area is constantly changing due to strong current surges, so a trough or channel may be present one year and sanded up the next. The water can be swift as well as deep, so be careful and wear your pfd.

b. On the Galveston side, fish **100-200 yards on either side of the water tower** that is 2.2 miles from the SLP bridge. **Exit 3005 at Rusty Hook Marina and turn right on the beach.**

11. San Luis Pass (SLP), Galveston Side. At the time of writing this book, the main channel of San Luis Pass is closer to the Galveston side than the **Follet Island** side. In fact, the main channel passes so close to the Galveston side, that most waders stay within ten to fifteen yards of the shoreline. No matter what time on the weekend I drive by the pass, there will be five to ten waders, plus others fishing from shore while sitting in lawn chairs. SLP is a popular place, no doubt about it, and for a good reason: after the Houston ship Channel, the pass is the largest thoroughfare for fish to enter and leave the Galveston Bay system. This includes not only speckled trout and red fish but also very large sharks. Just like other areas in the bay, fishing is usually best whenever the tides are moving. However, this also makes the pass a dangerous place to wade, so if you intend to be one of the waders, please wear your life vest because several people drown here every year.

12. Bait Camps.

    a. 8 Mile Road Bait Camp. 409-737-3457.

    b. Gulfside Seafood & Bait. 409-741-1360. (2nd bait shop on right on 61st street) Live bait.

    c. Angler's Bait. 409-744-9834. (3rd bait shop on right on 61st street) Live bait.

    d. Galvez Seafood Bait & Tackle. 409-741-2172. (4th bait shop on right on 61st street) Live bait.

    e. Pirates Beach Marina. 409-737-2592 (or 9966). Boat ramp, live bait.

    f. Rusty Hook. 409-737-2477. Live bait.

    g. Teakwood Marina on Tiki Island. 409-935-5552 or 281 -474-4954. Boat ramp, live bait.

    h. Tuckers Bait & Tackle. 409-741-8810. (1st bait shop on the right on 61st St.) Live bait.

    i. Uncle Buck's Bait Shop. 409-744-BAIT. (On the feeder, 50 yards before 61st St.) Live Bait.

    i. West Bay Bait and Tackle. 409-737-2908. Live bait.

    j. West Bay Marina. 409-737-3636. Boat ramp, live bait.

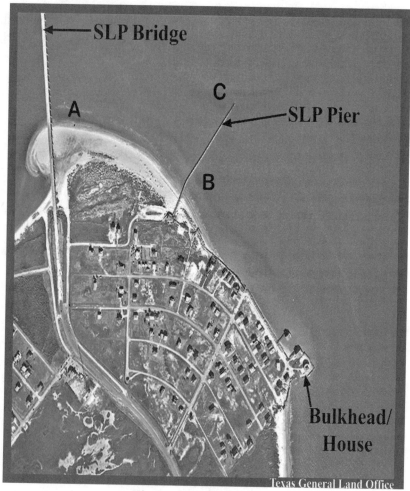

Figure 102. SLP Pier

San Luis Pass Area

1. San Luis Pass Pier. (979-233-6902). Open 24 hrs. Located on the Freeport side of the San Luis Pass Bridge. Take the 1st left after getting off the bridge and then another immediate left. No live bait is sold, but they have dead bait, tackle, restrooms and a grill. This pier is very popular under the lights at night, especially when word gets out that the trout are showing up on a tide change or when the red drum run starts.

Some places on the pier are better than others, so it is best to get there early in order to get the best spots. Look at **"B"** in **Figure 102**: on a high, incoming tide, fish either the first gut close to shore, that goes under the pier approximately where it bends to the south or try the second gut, which is about fifty to sixty feet past the bend. For the most part, the area around the pier has seen a lot of sand deposited and it is not as close to deep water as it once was. However, there are numerous cuts out near the end of the pier (See Figure 102 – "C") and a person should try to locate them to realize the full potential of fishing from this pier.

2. Fishing the Pass and behind Bird Island. The sandbar in the middle of the pass is a favorite spot of mine but the only time I fish this area is during the week because there is usually too much boat traffic on week ends. I usually launch my kayak from the beach area under the SLP Bridge on the west (**Follet Island**) side because it is easier to get to than the Galveston side, and I can get back on the main road faster to go home. I usually paddle straight out to the sandbar, right in the middle of the Pass. **To get to this beach, turn right immediately after leaving the bridge and then turn right again onto the road that parallels the Blue Water Highway (3005). On your left will be the entrance to the Brazoria County Park and boat launch (old KOA). Continue past this road and it will dead end at the beach. (See Figure 103)** The sand on the beach is hard except right at the end of the paved road as it enters the beach. A lot of people park and fish from the beach, however, at the present, it is shallow for a long way out. Any recent storm surge will dramatically change the depth and open up new channels that boaters and waders will have to learn. (See Figures 95, **100 – page C3, 101 – page C13, 104 – page C20**, and 110)

A lot of boats use the pass, so launching in this area has it's own special set of problems if you fish on the weekend. It can be similar to trying to walk across the race track during the Daytona 500. Once I reach the sandbar in the middle of the pass, I usually get off and wade, being sure to attach the kayak to me with a secure line.

113

Usually the water is only knee deep, even on the highest of tides and I will walk and fish both sides of this sandbar for almost 200-250 yards. The fishing can be great if the boat traffic is light, so it is usually not worthwhile at all on the week end. Please wear your pfd and be careful if the current is extremely strong; I have been on this bar at times when the sand would be literally sucked from under my feet. Another option is to paddle behind Bird Island and wade some of the guts that have been carved out during last summer's or this past winter's storms. This area changes every year so exact locations would not be accurate even six months later. You can easily find these deeper areas if the bay is fairly clear: look for water that is darker in color. I think of the larger gut being like a hand and I try to find the smaller guts that come off the larger gut like fingers on a hand. I have had a lot of good fishing experiences, wading these smaller guts in the back areas on an incoming tide even at noon in the summer. (See Figures 95 and 110)

Figure 103. Beach on Follet Isl. Side of San Luis Pass.

Caution! Two to three people drown in the SLP area almost every year because at certain times of the year, the current can be strong and treacherous. Wear your pfd in this area.

3. Titlum Tatlum Bayou. Located across Cold Pass, from the County Park (old KOA ramps). The mouth of the bayou is approximately 350 yards northeast of the ramp at the county park. On windy days it generally will hold green water. This bayou curves around and empties into where Christmas Bay and Bastrop Bay meet. The mouth of this bayou, at the southeast end, can be an exceptional place to fish on an outgoing tide. In the bayou there are several cuts or sloughs that feed into it and these can hold flounder or redfish. The one drawback that can ruin the fishing real fast is the boat traffic, so the best time to fish here is during the week. Go through the bayou slow if you are in a power boat because there are a lot of sand bars present. (See Figures 95, **104 – page C20**, 105, 108, 110, and 111)

The bayou looks like a three pronged pitch fork on the northwest end and the middle branch opens up into a small cove that at times can hold a large number of redfish. I usually get to this area by launching at **Cold Pass Marina,** however, at the present, the marina is only open to those who rent one of their cottages.

Mouth of Titlum Tatlum Bayou: 29.080 N, -95.138 W

4. Guyton Cut (Mud Cut) This is bayou that leads to **Bastrop Bay** and the mouth is 2 ½ miles north of the county park.

Mouth of Guyton Cut: 29.103 N, -95.158

5. Cold Pass.

a. The point of land in the far northeast corner of the county park is right next to a deep hole and it is also where **Cold Pass** and **SLP** come together. Launching either at the county park ramp or from the beach area close to the bridge, paddle approximately 50-100 yards out from the point. On days when the boat traffic is light and when there is a clean incoming tide, the fishing for specs and almost anything else that can be found in the surf, can be very good. I know a lot of people look down their nose at ladyfish, but catching one every now and then can be a lot of fun. My personal best ladyfish was caught in this area and it was almost three feet long and must have jumped six feet out of the water. (See Figures **104 – page C21**, 105, 108, 110, and 111)

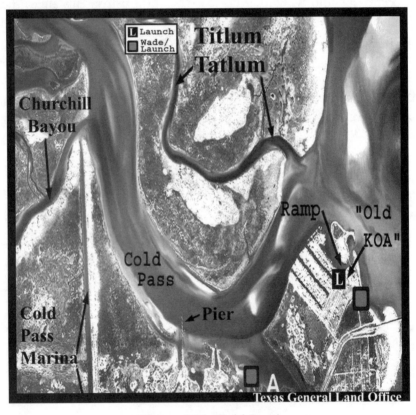

Figure 105. Cold Pass.

Turning left from the ramp will take you through Cold Pass to **Christmas Bay** and **Bastrop Bay**. Cold Pass makes a curve to the right and there is a large sand bar jutting out from the far shore. Most anglers in large boats, stay to the left of white PVC pipes in the middle of Cold Pass, however there is a cut close to the shore that could be used. (See Figure **104 – page C20**) In making this curve to the right you will probably see waders fishing on the left or south shoreline. These fishermen probably parked and waded out from a shallow cove just west of Brite Lite Grocery (See Figure **104 "A" – page C20**) and they are fishing the drop off along Cold Pass for flounder and specs. This is the first available spot after crossing the San Luis Pass Bridge, where anglers can park and fish **Cold Pass**. Turn off the road 0.7 miles past the bridge after you pass Bright Light Grocery. Be careful where you park, especially on a low tide.

There is a lot of deep mud lining the shoreline of the cove and it gets deeper as you get closer to mouth of the cove. The best way to enter the water to wade Cold Pass is to stay on dry land as much as possible and miss most of the mud in the cove, but there will still be mud along the shoreline of Cold Pass.

Figure 106. Pier in Cold Pass.

b. Just around the curve in Cold Pass you will see **a pier on the left**. This pier has shell plus some deeper areas around it. If you have a depth finder on your kayak, these and other holes and channels can easily be found with a little exploring. I have friends who catch reds around this pier almost every time they go out. (See Figure 106)

c. Churchill Bayou. This bayou is another way for kayakers to get to the north end of Cold Pass. The bayou is deep in places but the entrance to Cold Pass becomes very shallow. The south shoreline of Cold Pass next to the entrance of the canal from Cold Pass Marina, is an excellent area for wading; the bottom is hard sand and rocks. There is a house on the north bank where Churchill Bayou enters Christmas Bay and this gives a good visual fix while paddling across the bay. (See Figure 107)

Figure 107. Churchill Bayou to Sy's. Photo by Curley Myers.

twenty feet and these areas can hold fish in the heat of summer or in the cold of winter. You can find these deeper areas if you have a fishfinder on your kayak. In Churchill you will find several cuts that connect with Christmas Bay, and fish will use them to enter or leave the bay. In addition, they act as funnels pushing baitfish through as the tide ebbs and flows. Flounder and redfish will be drawn to the mouth of these cuts. (See Figures 109 "X" and **113 "D" – page C22**) If you are in something other than a kayak, play close attention to the maze of PVC pipe that marks the narrow channel from Sy's to Churchill in Christmas Bay. (See Figures **104 – page C20**, 105, 108, 110, and 111)

At the confluence of Cold Pass and Churchill Bayou, there is a channel takes you to **Cold Pass Marina**. The entrance to **Bastrop**

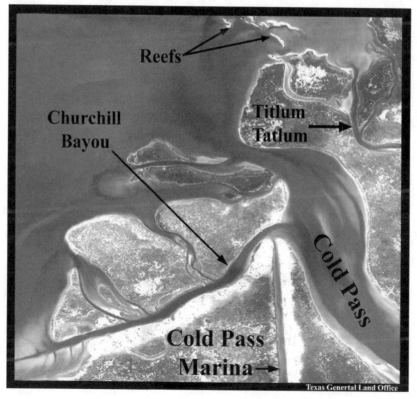

Figure 108. Cold Pass at Churchill Bayou.

119

Bay and Christmas Bay is further north. Both bays are shallow and there are a lot of oyster reefs, especially at the entrance to Bastrop Bay. I usually do not travel this far in a kayak, so I can not give any information about Bastrop Bay.

Figure 109. Churchill Bayou. Photo by Curley Myers.

4. Available boat ramps in the San Luis Pass area.

a. At the end of **Follets Island (Freeport side)** is Brazoria County Park. There are two ramps, side by side, however they are heavily used by motor boats. There are other places less congested that a kayaker can use. **800-3PARK RV, 979-233-6026,** Fax: **979-233-4433.** RV Hook-ups are $17/night for an inside spot; $20/night next to the water. They also have tent camping, showers, a laundromat and a small store, however the current management only allows customers renting the cottages to use all of the facilities.

b. Another place to launch your boat, with camping facilities is the **Cold Pass Marina, which is 1.8 miles from the end of the bridge.** Their ramp is located on a long canal which opens into where Churchill Bayou and Cold Pass come together. The marina canal gives easy access to not only the east shoreline of Christmas Bay, it is also just a short paddle to the northwest entrance of Titlum-Tatlum Bayou. The Cold Pass Marina has done a lot of renovation in the last year or so. They built three cabins that are different sizes and with prices ranging from $60 to $90/night. The units have everything except kitchens or running water. The facility is closed to everyone except to those who have reserved the cabins. **(979-239-2040).**

c. Sy's Bait Camp. This bait camp on Christmas Bay is reopening under new management and there is a public ramp at the end of the road. (See Figures 107, 111, and **112 – page C21, 113 – page C22**)

5. Sam's Pier (Fisherman's Warf Pier). This pier is 0.8 mile down the road from the light on Hwy. 332 where you turn onto the Blue Water Highway (3005). Look for a sign that says "Sam's Eff. Apt. and Pier". There is a parking lot but if you are going to park on the beach, there is a city fee. No live bait is sold.

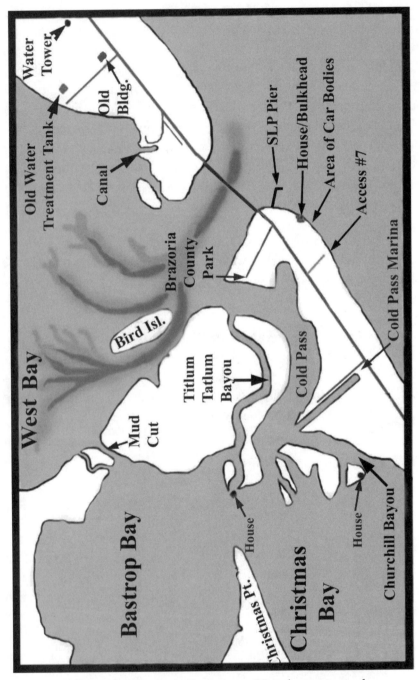

Figure 110. San Luis Pass Area. Not drawn to scale.

Christmas Bay

1. East Shoreline. Just north of Churchill Bayou, on the eastern edge of Christmas Bay, there is a marsh area that is shallow and made up mainly of reefs, sloughs, islands, and sandbars. In addition, there are smaller cuts leading to the major channels that should make excellent ambush points for flounder. (See Figure **113 "A" – page C22**)

This shoreline should be one of the best areas to fish in the Galveston Bay system but you must have a kayak to fish most of it. I do not see a lot of people fishing here, but it holds a lot of potential. **The best way to get to the east shoreline is by using Cold Pass Marina**, but since it is not always open, **the next best way is by launching at Sy's on the south shoreline**. (See Figures 107 and 111) This will take you through some prime fishing areas on the way to Churchill Bayou. When the wind is from the east, a good float plan would be to fish your way over to Churchill Bayou, starting at Sy's on the south shoreline, then fish the bayou for awhile, and let the wind help propel you back to where you started at the end of the day. This is what I try to do when fishing, every time I go out on the kayak, but sometimes the wind just doesn't cooperate.

2. Christmas Point Reef and the NW mouth of Titlum-Tatlum Bayou. It is located in the **northeast corner of the bay**. This is the entrance to Bastrop Bay, which has more reefs than any other bay I have ever seen at low tide. I have done very little fishing here. (See Figure 110 and **112 – page C21**)

To get to the NW mouth of Titlum-Tatlum Bayou, head NE in Cold Pass, and look for **an old house on stilts; the bayou is directly behind this house.** Fish the mouths of the three branches during an incoming tide for redfish and flounder. This area can be reached by kayak if you launch at Cold Pass Marina or from Sy's. Follow the pass as it curves to the northeast and a house on stilts will be the first one you encounter on the east shoreline. Enter the bayou on the right

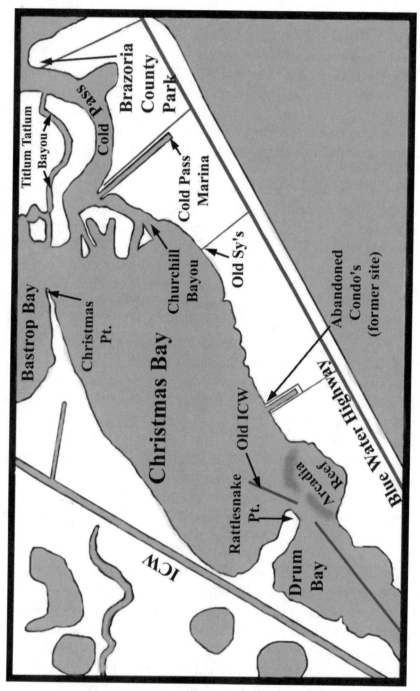

Figure 111. Christmas Bay. Not Drawn to Scale.

and in about 20-30 yards you will see on the left another branch of the bayou that opens up into a small cove; I will sometimes find large concentrations of rat reds in this cove.

3. South shoreline. There are many areas that should be tried on the south shoreline, and the angler should try each one because there will be differences in bottom structure along with differences in presence or absence of small coves or sloughs. Some of the dirt roads should not be attempted if there has been a recent rain or high tide. (See Figure **112 – page C21**)

    a. Sy's Bait Camp, which is opening under new management called Ernie's Too, is an excellent place to put in for either wade fishing or kayaking. This bait camp is 3.2 miles from the end of San Luis Pass Bridge (10 miles from the Surfside light). Wading to either the right or left can put you into the only area in the Galveston Bay Complex that is similar to the bays further south in that it has a large amount of sea grass growing 100-150 yards out from the shoreline. The bottom is mainly sand with mud occurring only in a few areas. You can see where the grass ends in the Figure **113 "B" – page C22**: notice the change in coloration. This a great interface to fish, for it allows predators to hide while waiting for unsuspecting baitfish. In addition, it also means that weedguards should be used with artificials. Also notice the sand bars close to the shoreline west of Sy's in Figure **113** **"C"**. In this same aerial photo, notice the very small cuts that occur where Churchill Bayou enters the bay. (Figure **113 "A"**) If you intend to wade to the west, start on the west side of the boat cut.

    b. Duck Blinds. 3.6 miles from the end of the San Luis Pass Bridge (9.6 miles form the light at Surfside) there is a dirt road which is right at the beginning of the S curves on the Blue Water Highway. (See Figure **113 "E" – page C22**) The road goes between several cedars and winds back to the bay where there is an area to park. Walk along a small stream to the bay and wade toward the duck blind. I believe this is one of the better walk-in places to fish, however it has become very popular lately.

c. Abandoned Condo's. (See Figures 111, **112 – page C21**, and 115) The condo's were torn down in early 2003 and I will have to say that even though they were an eyesore, I will miss the landmark. The road to this wading and launch site is 5.3 miles from the passbridge (7.9 miles from Surfside). Stay on the road that goes straight to the bay and do not turn right to the east side of the canal, which was the location of the condos; fishermen are not welcome. **To the left you can wade (paddle) to the entrance of Drum Bay** where the action can be very good on a fast outgoing tide. (See Figure **114 "C" – page C23**) As the water funnels out of Drum Bay bringing baitfish, flounder and reds will often be waiting. This bay is very shallow with a lot of oyster reefs, however it can at times have some excellent sight casting along the north and west shoreline. (See Figure **114 "E"**) While in the area of **Arcadia Reef**, it is just a short distance to **Rattlesnake Point**, a peninsula that makes up the northwest boundary of Christmas Bay. The shoreline is mainly shell and sand and it also offers a chance to possibly do some sight casting to red fish. (See Figure **114 "D"**)

Like the SE shoreline of Christmas Bay, there is a lot of grass along most of the area around the former Condo site. Two hundred yards out from the shoreline, there is a reef and unless you don't mind wading through deep mud, I suggest using a kayak.

Other areas that should be given close scrutiny would be the remnants of the **old intercoastal canal** (old ICW) that at one time ran through **Christmas Bay** and **Drum Bay**. (See Figure **114 "B"**) Most of the canal has sanded up over the years, however there are still a few deep areas that can be found with a depth finder. To the east of the former condo site, is a sand bar and a large slough that should be investigated. (See **Figure 114 "A"**)

Drum Bay and Swan Lake

Drum Bay is an area that I just started to explore last summer and it impressed me enough that I plan on spending a lot of time in the future getting to know this shallow bay system. (See Figures 111, **112 – page C21**, **114 – page C23**, 115, 116, 117, **118 – page C24**, and 119) Along with **Swan Lake**, Drum Bay is very shallow, consisting of a large number of oyster reefs with some areas having a sand bottom, and other areas that are thick with sea grass and a lot of deep mud. Although I have not found large concentrations, I have found that the shallow north shoreline can hold redfish to which I can sightcast. Another area to think about trying is **Nick's Lake**, which has all

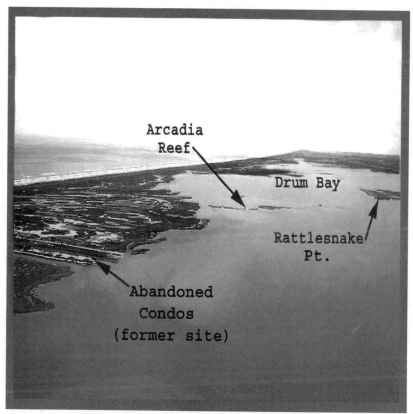

Figure 115. Christmas and Drum Bay.
Photo by Curley Myers.

127

the characteristics of other well known north shoreline lakes in West Bay, such as Green's. I have found that most people who I fish with, do not understand the basics of wading slow and quiet. There have been times while wading with friends, when almost all of the fish were scared out of the surrounding area shortly after we entered the water. **For a good discussion on wading, see Gary Wiist's article in the appendix.**

Another area that warrants exploring is the old intercoastal canal (ICW) that runs through Christmas Bay and Drum Bay. Although it is not used any more and most of the canal has become silted in, there are still deep areas in many places. Most of the sites mentioned in this section are within a reasonable paddle in a kayak.

Dirt and Shell Roads on Christmas Bay, Drum Bay and Swan Lake:

There are several drive-in/walk-in places that lead back to Christmas Bay, Drum Bay, and Swan Lake. Below are the approximate distances to each dirt road, from both the San Luis Pass Bridge and the Surfside Light. Please keep in mind that some of these roads are not used very much and sometimes they get overgrown, plus many of them are very muddy after either high tides or storms and they should not be attempted unless you have a four wheel drive vehicle.

0.7 mi. from SLP bridge = 12.4 mi. from Surfside light (cove behind Bright Lite and access to Cold Pass)

0.8 mi. from SLP bridge = 12.3 mi. from Surfside light

1.8 mi. from SLP bridge = 11.3 mi. from Surfside light (Cold Pass Marina)

3.1 mi. from SLP bridge = 10 mi. from Surfside light (Sy's Bait Camp which is now Ernie's Too)

3.6 mi. from SLP bridge = 9.5 mi. from Surfside light
(Duck blinds)

4.0 mi. from SLP bridge = 9.1 mi. from Surfside light

4.2 mi. from SLP bridge = 8.9 mi. from Surfside light
(mud road)

5.3 mi. from SLP bridge = 7.8 mi. from Surfside light
(former Abandoned Condos)

5.4 mi. from SLP bridge = 7.8 mi. from Surfside light
(not a dirt road but a slough close to the road and location
of communication tower)

Drum Bay starts about here

5.7 mi. from SLP bridge = 7.4 mi. from Surfside light

6.0 mi. from SLP bridge = 7.1 mi. from Surfside light

6.7 mi. from SLP bridge = 6.4 mi. from Surfside light

7.3 mi. from SLP bridge = 5.8 mi. from Surfside light

7.5 mi. from SLP bridge = 5.6 mi. from Surfside light

8.0 mi. from SLP bridge = 5.1 mi. from Surfside light

8.1 mi. from SLP bridge = 5.0 mi. from Surfside light

8.54 mi. from SLP bridge = 4.56 mi. from Surfside light
(ramp at end of road 257 F; very shallow with a lot of oyster
reefs; follow marked channel)

9.1 mi. from SLP bridge = 4.0 mi. from Surfside light
(10-15 yards to water)

Swan Lake starts here

10.9 mi. from SLP bridge = 2.2 mi. from Surfside light
(boat launch for ICW and Swan Lake)

11.02 mi. form SLP bridge = 2.08 mi. from Surfside light
(crabbing pier)

11.35 mi. from SLP bridge = 1.75 mi. from Surfside light
(water is 15- 20 yards away from 3005)

Figure 116. Drum Bay Reefs. Photo by Curley Myers.

Figure 117. Drum Bay. Photo by Curley Myers.

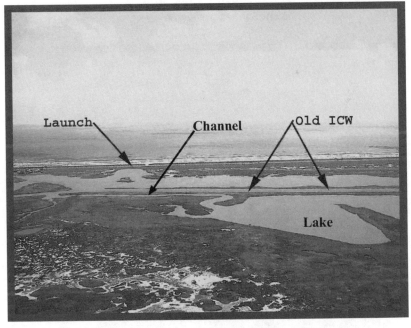

Figure 119. Lower End of Drum Bay.
Photo by Curley Myers.

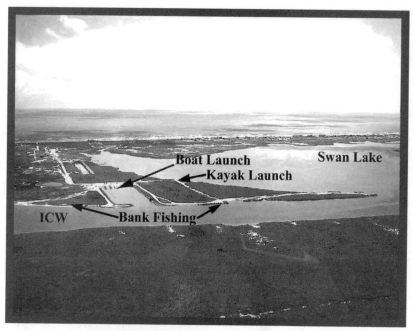

Figure 120. Boat Launch on East End of Swan Lake.
Photo by Curley Myers.

Figure 121. Swan Lake Kayak Launch Site.

Figure 122. Swan Lake

Marina's and Bait Shops:

Bright Lite Grocery. 979-233-8115. Live bait.

Ernies Too. 979-233-5159. Live bait. Boat launch.

Surfside

1. The following are the **distances to the access roads starting at the light at the base of the tall bridge in Surfside where 332 intersects the Blue Water Highway:**

1) **2.7 mi. = access rd. 1** (10.4 mi. from SLP bridge)

2) **4.0 mi. = access rd. 2** (9.1 mi. from SLP bridge)

3) **4.3 mi. = access rd. 3** (8.8 mi. from SLP bridge)

4) **5.3 mi. = access rd. 4** (7.8 mi. from SLP bridge)

5) **8.0 mi. = access rd. 5** (5.1 mi. from SLP bridge)

6) **10.0 mi. = access rd. 6** (3.1 mi. from SLP bridge)

7) **11.0 mi. = access rd. 7** (2.1 mi. from SLP bridge)

2. Bulkheads/house. Take beach road #7, which is 1.8 miles from the SLP bridge, and turn left. Drive down the beach until you end up at a house built on a bulkhead that sticks out in the water. The bulkhead holds bait and fish when the tides and wind are right. This area can be dangerous if you get too close to the bulkhead because the sand has been washed out from around the base of it and a large hole has been created. I do not know how common the name is, but I have heard of the washout being called the "dead man's hole". Fish at the base of the bulkhead for flounder. (See Figure 102)

3. Car Bodies. This "car reef" is located just west of the octagon house described in #2 and they are 30-50 feet out in the surf. Supposedly they were placed there by the former owner of the octagon house in the early 60's in an attempt to stop beach erosion around the house. This area can hold a lot of fish but be careful wading in the area because there can still be some rusted junk in the area.

4. Boilers. Where are they? According to the *Handbook of Texas Online*: www.tsha.utexas.edu/handbook/online/, the Acadia was an old Civil War steamship that was constructed as a blockade runner. She was a 738 tonner, 211 feet long, and built as a side-wheeler with a 900 horsepower engine. On Arcadia's first voyage in the area, she was run aground at night avoiding Union ships on February 6, 1865. The hull of the ship is now about 100-200 yards offshore due to shore erosion and she is protected by the Texas Antiquities Code.

The wreck has acted as a reef past the 3rd bar, however the boiler stacks have long since disappeared. Even so, there still may be enough of the wreck to warrant trying to locate it from a kayak, with a depth finder. I will admit that I do not know exactly where this wreck is located, but I will give you two locations that I have either heard or read about. (1) **Coming from Surfside, when the road gets as close to the beach as possible, the road makes an S curve and there are cedars on each side along with concrete and stone along the side of the road that prevents it from washing out. The wreck is located where the road just starts its curve on the surfside end.** (2) In a very old Joe Doggett article in the Chronicle, he implies that **it is located down from the Peregrine Condos which are found along the Blue Water Highway at Access Rd. #6.** Roy Merritt, in his book, *Introduction To Surf and Pier Fishing Along The Texas Coast* (page 39), concurs and gives the location as being **1.4 miles west of these same condos and 0.1 mile west of Access Road #5.** If you find it with a depth finder, you will have one super place to fish from a kayak.

135

5. Surfside Jetties. Directions. Coming from the Alvin/NASA area, take I-35 south out of Alvin and turn left on FM 523. Stay on 523 until you come to FM 332 and turn left. Take 332 and cross a high bridge over the ICW. An alternate route, coming from Texas City or other places south would be to take Hwy. 146 or I-45 to FM 646 and follow 646 until it dead ends on FM 2004. Turn right on 2004 and you will come to FM 523. Turn left onto 332. **If you are coming from Houston, take 228 south, and exit at Hwy. 332. Stay on 332 all the way to Surfside. Once over the bridge, turn right at the light onto Fort Valasco Rd. and continue until the road dead ends on Parkside Rd. (the very last road).** If you were to turn left at this same light, you would be on the Blue Water Highway and headed toward San Luis Pass. **Turn left on Parkside and you will see the Jetty Park on the right.** To launch a kayak, **turn left at the street before Parkside and this road will take you to the beach at the base of the jetties.** There are numerous bait shops along 332 if you want to use live bait. (See Figures 123 and 124)

Figure 123. Surfside Jetty.

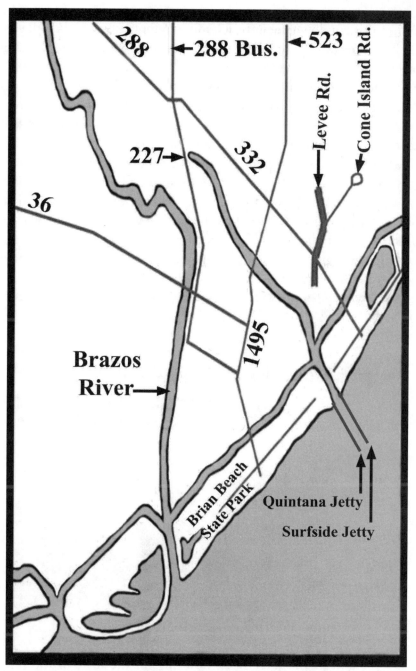

Figure 124. Brian Beach, Surfside and Quintana Jetties.
Not Drawn to Scale.

When walking down the jetty, look for anything unusual that may be sticking up from the granite, such as a metal pole or a 4x4 or a big piece of driftwood. These may have been put there by the regulars to mark their favorite spot. Try fishing on both sides of the "marker". If you want to fish close to the beach, look for an area where the waves do not break; this will be a deeper area called a "gut" between two sandbars. The 2nd gut is close to the large warning sign on the left side and the 3rd gut is about 35-40 steps past this sign.

These locations can change over time due to wave action, plus the guts are not as well defined as they are further down the beach. I hate giving away my favorite place to fish on this jetty, but if you look at Figures 127 "C" and 128 "C", there is a deep area about one fourth of the way down, that usually will hold a few specs.

Figure 125. Surfside Jetty Base, Channel Side.

North of the jetty park building, at the base of the jetty on the channel side, there is an L shaped area that can hold fish. Wading is difficult, due to a lot of large, odd shaped rocks in the water, however,

138

there is one large, flat rock that you can stand on and fish from, about fifteen feet from shore, close to the channel; the water here is about three feet deep next to the rock. I have seen very large trout caught in this area, and since it is adjacent to the ship channel, it should also be a great place for reds. (See Figure 125) If you look at Figures 127 "B" and 128 "B", you can see the structure that attract fish. There is a small pond at the north end of the jetty park and it drains into the channel to the left and above "B" in Figure 128. Notice the guts that have been carved into the sand to the left and right of "B". The rocks combined with the guts make this area a fish magnet.

One of my favorite ways to fish the jetty is to park at it's base and launch my kayak on the gulf side when the surf is calm. I usually paddle and troll out to the end and if the wind is from the SE, allow it to push the kayak down the side of the jetty about 50 yards out. This allows me to fish the rocks just as if I was bass fishing. I cast artificials up next to the rocks as I drift by and retrieve the lure at different speeds and different depths. I also like to paddle out to the end of the jetty and throw out a big spoon or jig and let the wind blow me back to the shore, all the time I'll be jigging and dragging that spoon up and down, right at the edge of the rocks at the bottom, most of the way to the beach; just be sure to hang on if a large red fish hammers it. Remember to be courteous to the rock walkers and don't infringe on their fishing area. Using a depth finder on your kayak, you can locate many large rocks that stick up from the bottom or depressions that you run across; this is when a GPS unit would come in handy. Once you know the underwater structure, fishing from the jetty itself will be a lot more productive.

About 50-75 yards down from the base of the jetty, you can park right next to the channel and fish. **Directions: Instead of turning left to go to the Surfside Jetty Parking, continue straight and there will be a dirt road that will take you to the Freeport Channel.** (See Figures 126 and 128 "A") This shoreline allows a person to fish out of the back of his car since he can park right next to the channel.

Figure 126. Freeport Channel

Surfside Jetty Park. 979-239-3547. The park building has restrooms on the second level and outdoor showers on the ground floor. A small store sells picnic items but they do not sell bait.

Figure 127. Surfside and Quintana Jetties.

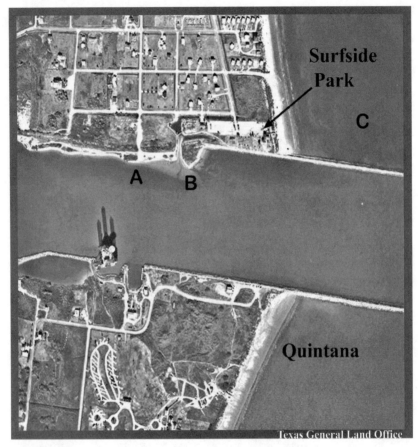

Figure 128. Surfside/Quintana Jetties.

Quintana Jetty & Brazos River Area

1. Quintana Jetties. Directions: From the NASA area take 35 south out of Alvin and turn left on 523. Continue on 523 past the turnoff to surfside (332) for approximately two miles and 1495 will branch off to the left. **If you are coming from Houston,** take 288 Business and it dead ends at 495 where you will turn right. However it would be quicker to stay on 288 (not the business route) and after it turns into 332 it will cross 288B, where you will turn right.1495 will go over the ICW. Turn left on 723 (Lamar St.) at the stop sign, right on 5th St., left on Barnet St. and right on 2nd St. Stay on 2nd St. and it will take you to the base of the Quintana Jetty. I do not fish this jetty often, simply because it is a longer drive for me and the water on the gulf side of this jetty always seems to be muddy. The main attraction, however, is the smaller number of people that fish on it. (See Figures 127 and 128) **Quintana Beach Park and Pier** are in this same area, however the pier does not extend out into very deep water so a person could stand on the beach and cast just about as far.

2. Canals Close to Quintana Jetties. This area can be good when the water in the ICW is clear. Once you **go across the intercoastal swing bridge** the **canals are on the left.** After **turning left at the stop sign, turn after 20 yards into the first dirt road or go down one block and turn left and find a place to park.** These canals were built and bulk headed for a development that was never completed.

3. Bryan Beach and Brazos River Mouth. Directions: 1495 will dead end at the beach. Look for signs that say **Bryan Beach and Quintana Jetties. When you get to the surf, turn right and follow the beach all the way to the mouth of the Brazos; most of this beach "road" is well maintained.** This is the **Bryan Beach Recreation Area.** There is a shrimp boat stranded on the second bar in the surf 0.5 miles from where 1495 dead ends at the beach. Make note of this location for future reference because at some point in time, that boat will be 100 or more yards offshore.

Fishing at the mouth of the Brazos River can be outstanding as long as there has not been a lot of rain and fresh water run off. The best spot is usually right where the breakers and the river intersect. At the end of the beach road, there is an area of backwater that is a good place to catch bait. Fish to the left of the mouth with surf rods for bull reds and sharks and fish the flats along the river channel for trout and flounder. (See Figure 129)

Figure 129. Brazos River Mouth.

Appendix A

Wade and Kayak Fishing in Galveston and Surrounding Areas, 3rd Ed.*

May be purchased by sending check or money order for $19.45 plus $4.50 for tax and shipping to:

Ray Crawford
702 Balmoral Ct.
Friendswood, TX 77546

Flyfisher@ev1.net (E-V-one)
Website: www.geocities.com/fishing_honey_holes/

*Formally *Honey Holes: Galveston Bay and Surrounding Areas for Walk-in Waders and Kayakers*

Appendix B

Wade Smart by Gary Wiist

Two things which are keys to successful wading are stealth, and safety. Stingrays are plentiful in Gulf Coast waters, so you must always consider that there may be one where your next step is about to fall. Getting stuck by a ray, even if only a "minor" strike, is a sure end to the day's fishing for all but the most hardy. The wounds are not only quite painful, but also very prone to infection, so they should be treated by a doctor as soon as possible. To minimize the pain until such time, the usual recommended procedure is to run hot water over the wound. If you are in a boat, the exhaust water from the motor is usually warm enough to make a difference in the pain level. I have been fortunate enough to avoid testing this theory on myself, but have been around a few people when they needed to do so, and it seems to help.

Wading conditions on our coast vary widely from area to area. The one thing which is consistent is that you can find a variety of bottom types in each of our bay systems. There are areas of firm bottom, areas of extremely soft bottom, and everything in between. Wading can be a very relaxing method of fishing, and is often more productive than staying in the boat, particularly for large trout in shallow water. The following methods are some that I have used to help insure my safety, and keep me quiet enough to get close to shallow water fish.

Wading truly quietly is in itself a sort of an art form. You must learn to do so in a variety of bottom conditions to effectively sightcast with regular success. The most important thing overall is to move slowly. This does not mean just your overall forward progress, but the speed with which you move your feet through the water as well. If you can hear yourself, you are going way too fast. If you can see much of a bulge in the water in front of your foot, you are still going too fast. I think perhaps the best image to impart this is to think in terms of moving as if you have been videotaped and are being played back in very slow motion. A key to this slow wading is to always keep your weight on the planted foot until the foot that is moving, finds a good place to land, THEN allow your weight to shift forward. I move my foot with the toes never leaving contact with the bottom, using the toe of my shoe as a probe. If you try to wade as you normally walk, your weight is shifting as your feet are moving, and this will cause you to be a lot noisier, especially in areas where the bottom firmness and/or contours are not consistent. My method allows you to keep your balance while your foot has time to explore the bottom prior to you putting your weight on it. It gives you some warning when you are about to hit a soft spot, rather than be surprised by it and thus lurch forward. I prefer to wade in tennis shoes with a stout but flexible bottom. This allow me much more feel of the bottom contour and texture than wearing something with a very stiff sole, but provides enough protection to prevent slices from oysters, glass, or other debris you may encounter. My old Red Ball waders are boot waders, and I find they are much more difficult for me to be quiet in due to the stiffness of the boots. I now mainly use stocking foot neoprenes in the winter and wear oversized tennis shoes to accommodate the extra bulk.

I think the combination of slow movement, and keeping your weight back is also key in avoiding trapping a ray with your foot and risking a very painful reminder that you are wading improperly. If you are moving your feet extremely slow and your toes have constant contact with the bottom, you will prod the ray with your shoe toe, and it has plenty of time to get off the bottom and move. If you are moving faster and shifting your weight as you move, or do so with your toes raised, you can slide your foot onto the ray and put your weight on it before the ray has had time to flee. I've watched many rays (and even experimented with them some) in clear water, and I have never seen one that would not leave if I gave it the chance. I have had many people tell me that they or their friends were "wading correctly" but got stuck anyway. Invariably, those that I've had an opportunity to later observe in the water were wading fast enough tohave met with the circumstances I just described, or they keep only the heel and back portion of their feet on bottom, raising the toe as they move.

Another thing to be careful about is losing your balance and stepping backward. I was fishing with a guy for the first time a couple of years ago, and we pulled his boat up near some marsh. I waded toward the shoreline, intending to go over it to some slough areas behind it, and he was right behind me. He lost his balance in a depression and stepped backward right onto a ray, which wasted no time in letting him know it was there in a rather painful manner. Again, keeping your weight on the back foot until the other finds solid footing helps prevent this occurrence. Rays will sometimes follow a person wading, eating things that are disrupted from the bottom or grass by the wader, so stepping backward can be a risky proposition.

The above method works great on a sand flat or other firm bottom, but what about the mud and clay bottoms? These bottom types add an additional challenge to your effort to be quiet. The mud allows your feet to sink, often well up toward your knees or worse. This has a major tendency to cause you to create fairly loud sucking or slurping sounds as you retrieve your foot, and it also tends to make you want to shift your weight sooner than you might prefer. One thing I do to help alleviate this is to twist my foot as I raise it, bringing it up toes last. This breaks the suction by changing the angle of your foot to the hole it has created, allowing water to enter along the sides of your foot as you move it upward. This keeps the water from rushing in all at once after you raise your foot to the top of the hole and thus alleviating the sucking sound. To help with the lack of balance the softness creates, I utilize the fact that I am keeping my weight on the back foot, and search for the firmest spots I can locate, sometimes finding shell or other debris in the mud to keep me from sinking as far. Clay type bottoms frequently have the greatest suction effect, even though they are generally firmer and you don't sink as far into them. The same slight twisting of the foot helps to break it loose without causing a lot of noise, and you can readily feel when it has released from the bottom. Grass beds present their own challenges as well. In many of the grasses along our coast, if you follow the above suggestions and keep your feet in contact with the bottom, it isn't long before you are dragging around a considerable weight of grass wrapped around your ankles. The bulk of the grass is not only a problem due to the weight, but also because it provides a much larger surface area to push a wake in front of your feet as they move. The quiet way to overcome this is to lift your foot slowly, tilting it so that your toes leave the water last. Allow the grass to slide off, then reenter the water with your foot slowly, toes first to avoid a "plop". Angling your foot as you lift it also helps avoid lifting the grass mat out of the water and allowing it to splat back down. Putting your foot right back where it came from is advisable, as putting it elsewhere in the grass puts you at risk to rays. If you have been seeing a lot of rays and/or are in an area where your wading is muddying up the water so you can't see the bottom and are thus uncomfortable about it, slide your foot, toes first, down your other leg to the bottom, and then across the area where you intend to place it to check for rays prior to putting your weight on it. Do NOT forget to drag your feet in any water where you cannot clearly determine that there is not a ray where you are about to put your foot.

I certainly cannot offer you any guarantees, but this has worked for me for over 30 years of wading bays. If you employ the ideas I've presented here you will find that you can wade quietly and safely. You will have to concentrate to do so at first, but with practice it will become second nature for you, and I'll bet you find yourself catching more fish too!!

Appendix C

References:

1. "**Fishing the Texas Gulf Coast and Bays Without a Boat, 2nd Ed.**", 1999, by Roy K. Merritt. An excellent resource for the entire Texas Gulf Coast.

2. "**Fly Fishing the Texas Coast: Backcountry Flats to Bluewater**", 1999, by Chuck Scates and Phil H. Shook. A detailed look at all aspects of saltwater fly fishing, along with coverage of the Texas Gulf Coast.

3. "**Pocket Guide to Speckled Trout and Redfish: Upper Coast Edition**", 1990, by George Meason and Greg Cubbison. A very good look at equipment to use and where to fish.

4. "**Saltwater Strategies: How, When and Where to Fish the Western Gulf Coast**", 1998, by Larry Bozka. This book covers everything from equipment, to knots, to strategies to use at different locations along the Texas Gulf Coast.

5. "**The Original Guide to Family Fishing Holes Within 120 Miles of Downtown Houston, 8th Ed.**", 2003, by Lorraine Leavell. An excellent description of saltwater and freshwater fishing locations along with maps.

Appendix D

Bait Camps and Marinas

3 Amigo's, 281-474-7447
8-Mile Rd. Bait Camp, 409-737-1003
50-50 Bait and Tackle, 409-945-2506
Angler's Bait, 409-744-9834
Anita's Bait, Tackle, and Seafood, 409-945-5727
Bait Shack, 979-233-7070
Basin Bait Camp, 409-762-3168
Beach Bait and Tackle, 979-233-7351
Bolivar Bait Camp, 409-684-4210
Boyd's 1 Stop, 409-945-4001
Bridge Bait & Tackle, 979-239-2248
Brite Lite Grocery, 979-233-8115
Cold Pass Marina, 979-239-2040
Crawley's Bait Camp, 281-383-3665
Curl's Fisherman Headquarters, 409-948-3894
Dollar Point Bait Camp, 409-945-4808
Eagle Point Marina, 281-339-1131
Ernie's Bait Camp, 979-233-6250
Ernie's Too, 979-233-5159
Falcon Seafood Co, 409-684-3838
Fat Boys, 409-935-4151
Galveston Bait and Tackle, 409-740-1185
Galvez Seafood Bait & Tackle, 409-741-2172
Gulfside Seafood and Bait, 409-741-1360
Jay Woody's, 409-355-2308
Lea's Bait and Tackle, 409-945-5675
Linda's at Sylvan Beach, 281-471-5705
Louis Bait Camp, 409-935-9050
Nash's Bait Camp,
Pirates Beach Marina, 409-737-2592 or 409-737-9966

Ray's Marina and Bait Camp, 409-945-0989
Rock Bottom Bait & Tackle, 409-684-7224
Rollover Pass Bait and Tackle, 409-286-5562
Rusty Hook, 409-737-2477
Salygrass Bait and Tackle, 979-239-3650
San Leon Marina, 281-339-1515
Shirley's Bait Camp, 409-684-8251
Smitty's, 409-744-7705 or 409-744-9049
Spillway Bait and Tackle, 281-559-2403
Stingaree Marina, 409-684-9530
T.C.'s Bait Camp, 281-559-1231
Teakwood Marina, 409-935-5552 or 281-474-4454
Tim's Bait & Tackle, 409-286-5693
The Baiten Place, 409-744-9152
Thompson's Fishing Camp, 281-427-2300
Tucker's Bait and Tackle, 409-741-8810
Uncle Buck's Bait Shop, 409 737-2908
Way Out Marina, 409-684-3070
West Bay Bait and Tackle, 409-737-2908
West Bay Marina, 409-737-3636

Index

Wade and Kayak Fishing